WITHDRAWN

JAYAPRAKASH NARAYAN

A Political Biography

Ajit Bhattacharjea

Revised and Updated

VIKAS PUBLISHING HOUSE PVT LTD
New Delhi Bombay Bangalore Calcutta Kanpur

DS
481
N3
B45
1978

Paper used for printing of this book was made available by the Government of India at concessional rates

Bell Books
Paperback Division of
Vikas Publishing House Pvt Ltd

© AJIT BHATTACHARJEA, 1975

Cover Sketch by R. K. LAXMAN

First Bell Books edition, 1978

Printed at Modern Printers, K-30, Navin Shahdara, Delhi 110032

*To my son Aditya without whose research
assistance and quiet enthusiasm
this book would have taken
many more months*

PREFACE

THIS MONTH, the movement guided by Jayaprakash Narayan in Bihar is a year old. It has already lasted longer and spread further than most observers expected. Whatever the outcome, its place in history is assured. Yet only a year ago Bihar seemed condemned to remain the most corrupt, backward and apathetic State in the Union; and JP was vaguely remembered as having once been considered a possible successor to Jawaharlal Nehru as Prime Minister. But then he had buried himself for 20 years in a visionary project for voluntary redistribution of land and renounced party politics. Today these apparently inert elements have fused to produce the biggest movement for social and political reform since independence.

The movement is no longer confined to Bihar. Other States have similar problems and the same desire for change. Most worried of all are those in power in New Delhi because the emergence of new socio-political forces in the country imperils their future, and they have the most to lose. That is why a confrontation between JP and the Prime Minister was inevitable.

The wide response that JP has evoked is an index of the widespread concern in the country about the way it is being ruled and the yearning for a leadership whose honesty is beyond doubt. It is a reflection of lack of confidence in all levels of government. JP offers no panaceas. Nor is he a good orator. In fact, at times he can be as tedious as a teacher trying to make sure that the dullest student in the class understands the lesson. He has written brilliant tracts on politics but that was long ago. People flock to him today because of his patent sincerity: he has captured the credibility that the politicians have lost.

What does this mean for India? Nothing much if JP had been

just another party leader, for then he would have had to function within the same political constraints. But what makes him unique is the absence of any desire to wield power; therefore he cannot be tempted by it. His concern is with values, not votes. He is more a Gandhi than a Nehru. What are his values and objectives? JP has written, spoken and worked so much in the field of politics that a comprehensive and definitive biography would fill several volumes and take years to write. This book is a limited, selective and hurried attempt to provide some insight into the development of his political thinking as a background to the Bihar movement and what may follow. The reader will find that JP has changed ideologies but not values. In fact, he is more a teacher of political science on a mass scale than a politician wanting to wield power.

I would like to take this opportunity to thank the many people who came forward to help so readily when they heard that I was writing on JP. The Nehru Memorial Library and the Gandhi Peace Foundation in New Delhi and the Meherally Centre in Bombay have been of particular assistance. But if any mistakes have been committed or any vital developments overlooked, the fault is entirely my own.

AJIT BHATTACHARJEA

New Delhi
March 1975

PREFACE TO THE REVISED EDITION

THE CONCLUDING chapter of the first edition of this book, completed in March 1975, was entitled "Back to Struggle." It ended with a quotation from a statement by Jayaprakash Narayan provoked by the significant increase in the level of police brutality used to put down the movement organized by the students of Bihar against corruption, high prices and unemployment, and for basic and long overdue changes in the educational system. The orders to step up the level of repression had obviously come from New Delhi. JP then warned: "Those who think that sarvodaya is made up of goody-goody people, who no doubt talk about non-violent revolution but do not mean it seriously, are in for a surprise. Speaking for myself, I cannot remain a silent spectator to misgovernment, corruption and the rest, whether in Patna, Delhi or elsewhere. It is not for this that I had fought for freedom...I have decided to fight corruption, misgovernment and blackmarketing, profiteering and hoarding, to fight for the overhaul of the educational system, and for real people's democracy."

Nobody, not even JP himself, quite realised at the time how rapidly conflict would escalate, how near it would take India to dictatorial rule; or the role he would play, despite a crippling sickness incurred in jail and its impact on his mental faculties, in activating popular reaction against an increasingly callous and cruel administration and thus guiding the country back towards democratic freedoms. He made mistakes and miscalculations, but the belief at the core of his faith was shown to be fully justified. This was that if the issue was posed clearly, the moral sense and political values instilled in the average poor and illiterate citizen of the country would make him opt unhesitatingly for a free and open society and a representative form of government. In fact, he predicted the form the electoral contest would take more than two years before it was held. The cynics and courtiers surrounding Prime Minister Indira Gandhi did not share this belief and thus allowed a general election to take place which swept them from power.

These lines are being written after JP has returned once again to his modest, lonely home in Patna after seven weeks in Bombay and three in the United States for treatment to arrest the painful and debilitating effect of his dependence on dialysis three times a week, to stay alive. His condition has not improved despite a dramatic dash half-way around the globe to a Seattle hospital to ease the painful process of linking his shrinking blood vessels to an artificial kidney machine. He remains as dependent on it as before. He had stayed in Bombay to be near expert medical assistance and modern hospital equipment, but there was no stable improvement in his condition, which varied from day to day. On medical advice, he had lived in a luxurious penthouse apartment provided by his friend, Ramnath Goenka, above the *Indian Express* skyscraper to get as much rest as possible. But he was isolated there from the crucial political developments that would determine India's future and from the common people he had identified himself with for so long. He was surviving on will power and his concern for his country; so he returned to Patna once again, the capital of a State that represented more vividly than any other all that had gone wrong in the thirty years of Congress rule after India became independent.

He was nearing 75 and found it hard to bear the repeated shouts of "Lok Nayak Zindabad" and other slogans, and the heavy garlands placed on him. He was also taken in more easily than before by visitors seeking recommendations and favours. Patna was as dirty as ever; men, women and children still slept on the pavements, ragged pieces of cloth or jute their only protection against the monsoon rain. What, then, had been achieved?

Spurning, as always, power or political office, JP could only hope to influence events by his ability to arouse public opinion. He had turned down a proposal that he be nominated for election as President of the Republic though there was no doubt that he would have been elected if he had agreed to stand. Although the ruling Janata party owed its electoral victory primarily to him, most of its leaders would have preferred him to be confined within the formal trappings of this largely ceremonial office to avert embarrassment. Some had come to the point of regarding him as an enfeebled crank whom they could not afford to antagonise publicly. It was as if the calendar had gone back thirty years, with the leaders of a newly-independent India embarrassed by the views and reactions of Mahatma Gandhi who had led them to freedom but could not conceal his unhappiness with the lust for power that grew among them; their uncritical acceptance of foreign political, economic and social models, especially from the West and the Soviet Union; and their inability to fashion, even consider, indigenous remedies for indigenous problems that were so different in nature to those faced by foreign countries. JP did not have the health or the discipline that the Mahatma still retained, in 1957; but he had the same vision, the same empathy with the rural poor and the same ability to break out of the limitations of a rigid ideology or system and seek ways to promote new processes leading towards greater freedom and self-reliance, and minimising dependence on the government. He was greater than Gandhi, perhaps, in his vision of, and commitment to, freedom in the widest sense of the word. Throughout his life, any threat to freedom, anywhere, provoked an instant response from him.

That was the cause of the agony and self-doubt expressed in

his *Prison Diary* when he found that the mass movement he had encouraged and guided in an effort to make the poorest and most under-privileged Indian aware and jealous of his rights, had in fact provided the Indira Gandhi government with an excuse to impose a more authoritarian and callous form of government on the country than it had experienced even under colonial rule. The limited reaction against this move towards despotism, even when its nature became clear by the steps taken to transfer supreme power to her second son, Sanjay, made him wonder whether he had overrated the average Indian's commitment to a free society. But he never lost faith entirely, and continued his efforts to unite the non-communist Opposition parties and to prepare the people to vote against authoritarianism when the opportunity arose. Few of his friends and colleagues were able to retain the same faith or hope for such an opportunity. They urged him to be more realistic. It was JP's faith and prescience however that won out in the end.

But that was not the end; at best a new process had begun. The new Janata ministers were not impervious to the corrupting influence of power and patronage, magnified so many times over in a poor country. And so the struggle to create and strengthen counter-balancing institutions and new, uncorrupted channels through which the under-privileged could impress their demands on the government, continued.

The present edition of JP's political biography has been revised and updated to cover the main developments occurring between the start of the Bihar movement and the election of the Janata party and government.

AJIT BHATTACHARJEA

New Delhi
October 1977

CONTENTS

One	ROOTS OF STRUGGLE	1
Two	EARLY YEARS	31
Three	AMERICA AND MARXISM	41
Four	THE YOUNG CONGRESSMAN	54
Five	CSP—BIRTH OF A PARTY	62
Six	THE COMMUNIST BETRAYAL	74
Seven	QUIT INDIA	87
Eight	BREAK WITH CONGRESS	106
Nine	STRAINS AMONG SOCIALISTS	126
Ten	THE BHOODAN YEARS	146
Eleven	ALTERNATIVES TO VIOLENCE	159
Twelve	BACK TO STRUGGLE	171
Thirteen	THE BIHAR MOVEMENT	176
Fourteen	DESPAIR AND HOPE	196
Fifteen	THE CONTINUING SEARCH	220

Freedom, with the passing of the years transcended the mere freedom of my country and embraced freedom of man everywhere and from every sort of trammel—above all it meant freedom of the human personality, freedom of the mind, freedom of the spirit. This freedom has become a passion of life, and I shall not see it compromised for bread, for power, for security, for prosperity, for the glory of the State or for anything else.

—JAYAPRAKASH NARAYAN

CHAPTER ONE
ROOTS OF STRUGGLE

EVERY ROAD had been travelled before. Each village was familiar. Once again the rivers were in spate in north Bihar in August, huts marooned, crops destroyed, at places the flood seemed to stretch to the Himalayan foothills from where the Gandak, the Kosi and 20 other rivers poured melted snow and monsoon water into the broad Gangetic plain. As so often before, village families were carrying whatever they could rescue to higher ground. Others waited in their marooned mud huts for the flood to subside. It could take weeks. Few knew that millions had been sanctioned for flood-protection works in the previous 25 years. Those who did, also knew enough of corruption to shrug their shoulders. Only the buffaloes and the children riding them into the water looked happy—when they were not too hungry. South of the swollen Ganga, not 50 miles away, rainfall had been poor, the crops were turning yellow and local rivers were still muddy streams. That, too, was the Bihar he knew.

Tubewells and the transmission lines serving them were the only new features on the landscape. But they looked silly surrounded by floodwaters. And in the south, where they were needed, power supply was irregular, often coming on only at night. The ambitious Damodar Valley Corporation, modelled on America's well known Tennessee Valley Authority, was proving another disappointment—it had not tamed the river, nor was it generating the power expected.

Otherwise, he could well have been travelling there more than four decades earlier, when he had first toured the country intensively to establish the Congress Socialist Party, a group formed with some of the best young minds of the time—Ram

Manohar Lohia, Asoka Mehta, Minoo Masani, Yusuf Meharally, Achyut Patwardhan—to try and inject the conservative lawyer-dominated freedom movement with Marxist activism. It was an outstanding group, responding with intelligence, sensitivity, and knowledge of political development abroad to the contrary attractions of power and morality that have agonized our times, symbolized for them by the teachings of Gandhi and Marx. He was an avowed Marxist at the time, fresh from radical associations on American campuses. But the pull that the struggle for independence exerted on his emotions had proved far stronger than the intellectual appeal of a foreign ideology and, chip by chip, the realities of India eroded his attachment to Marxist dogma. He joined the Indian National Congress instead of the Communist Party of India. Soon he was appointed acting general secretary of the Congress and followed other leaders to jail. Tall, strikingly handsome, combining intellectual brilliance with human sentiment, writing in English with a clarity that rivalled Nehru's, he had soon attracted the attention of Jawaharlal, 13 years his senior. His Hindi was even better, in spite of seven years in the United States. He could sit on the floor with the remotest villager, especially from his home province, for he came from a poor middle class family and was at home even in the native Bhojpuri dialect.

Or the time could have been January 1934, when he took part in his first relief operation to help victims of the disastrous Bihar earthquake. (In later years, frequent droughts and floods gave full scope to his talent for attracting volunteers and donations.) Or 1942, when, escaping from Hazaribagh jail, he organized an armed guerrilla campaign against the British colonial regime that made him an instant hero of every student frustrated by Mahatma Gandhi's insistence on non-violence. He was rearrested. But when he emerged from prison on the eve of independence, it was Gandhi who suggested he become president of the Congress Party so that his countrywide popularity, next only to Nehru's, could be used to unite and inspire the party when its senior leaders yielded to the temptations of ministerial office. And, possibly, also because his village-oriented, non-elitist attitude could provide a corrective to the far from revolutionary ease with which Nehru slipped into the shoes of the defunct British Raj in his Fabian commitment to state socialism and industrialization. But Nehru and the established Congress leadership reacted negatively and a tired and disillusioned Gandhi did not insist.

Or it could have been later, when he was touring Bihar in the early fifties to campaign unsuccessfully for candidates put up by a separate Socialist Party formed when he and his colleagues found it impossible to function within the Congress after independence. Despite the breach, he was regarded as the next Prime Minister, and was invited to join the cabinet. But he turned down the offer when Nehru refused to commit himself to a specific minimum programme. The Socialist Party, too, almost split on the issue, with Ram Manohar Lohia insisting that there should be no compromise with the Congress. And then the new party had proved no match for the Congress in organizing ability or in raising money. It had split completely thereafter, as parties formed by uncompromising intellectuals so often do.

It was about this time, too, that he lost faith in the Westminster-style parliamentary system that India had lifted, with very few changes, from Britain. He had been sceptical about it for a long time. The first general election held in 1952 under India's new republican constitution confirmed his doubts. The temptation to indulge in demagoguery—excite sectarian passions, tell halftruths, make impossible promises, and spend huge sums in the process—proved to be overwhelming with an illiterate and fragmented electorate. What made things worse was the fact that the bigger and more successful parties had little internal democracy. They were run by a small clique of bosses, and it was they who nominated and financed party candidates.

Another ideological watershed crossed in the fifties concerned the role of state power. Fascism he had rejected much earlier, but the experience of Soviet Russia showed him that irrespective of the ideals inspiring communism, a strong state apparatus that treated all opposition as treason, led to dictatorship and tyranny, not freedom in any sense. The last variation of a state-dominated economic and political system in which he lost faith was the welfare state which he found destructive of local initiative, encouraging dependence on a remote and corruptible elite. This was equally subversive of democracy which he viewed as a system that encouraged the individual, and even more than the individual the community, to develop according to its own native genius. And so he came to accept fully the Gandhian preference for minimum government and maximum independent community initiative.

He did not give up his socialist stance or his interest in political developments. The reasons he gave for his withdrawal from party and power politics in a letter to his party colleagues in 1957 illustrate the clarity of his thinking. After describing the process of realization that reliance on state power inevitably involves curtailment of freedom, he defined his goal, which was "to create and develop forms of socialist living through the voluntary endeavour of the people rather than seek to establish socialism by the use of the power of the state. In other words, the remedy is to establish people's socialism rather than state socialism." Seven years later, this commitment was put to test. Nehru was ailing. The end was near when his closest colleague in the cabinet—and the man who in fact would succeed him as Prime Minister—the modest but capable Lal Bahadur Shastri, approached JP. The proposal was that JP should be the next Prime Minister. But he was not tempted.

He also resented the individualism on which the one-man-one-vote principle was based and feared it would atomize Indian society as it had done in the West, reducing the individual to "a grain of sand in a sand heap," alienated from his family and social environment. He felt certain that a community approach to social change and to the choice of legislators would suit the country better if the village community was shorn of its traditional injustices. (Unlike the Nehru brand of socialists, he thought in rural rather than urban terms.) And so he began to put more stress on the idea of a "communitarian society" on the village-panchayat pattern in which the individual would function like "a living cell in a living organization," and of a "partyless democracy" in which the primary unit would take decisions by consensus and delegate powers for regional, national, and international functions to secondary units. Political parties, in the sense of power groups, would, therefore, have no role to play. He had come to this thesis by analyzing the defects of industrialized Western societies and hoped it was not too late for India to adopt a different course.

His new conviction brought him even closer to the people. And so the current tour could have been taking place at any time in the last 20 years, after he had finally left party politics to plunge into the *bhoodan* (voluntary land-sharing) movement sponsored by Acharya Vinoba Bhave, widely accepted as Gandhi's spiritual heir. Following the honoured tradition of selfless, inward-looking seers and prophets, Vinoba Bhave had emphasized the spiritual aspect of the Mahatma's legacy, depending exclusively on conversion, rejecting any form of coercion. He had worked out an entire technique and model of comprehensive social change based on voluntary sharing and self-regulating village units.

Since scarcity of land was the most widespread problem in a basically rural society, he began by asking landowners to contribute a small portion of their lands to the landless. Subsequently they were expected to pledge all their land to the village but continue to hold it in trust. Others participated by contributing, according to their method of livelihood, a portion of their wages, produce, or labour. A village council consisting of all the adults took decisions by unanimity or at least consensus (to avoid politicking). The village councils also formed the base units for a system of indirect elections to regional, state and, ultimately, national assemblies.

Vinoba's own efforts—he had walked thousands of miles to propagate his doctrine—had evoked a fair degree of response from landowners, especially in areas threatened by violence. Much support from the government (which was only too happy to shake off the responsibility of land reform) had given a fair measure of credibility to the programme. It also provided an rscape from the petty jealousies and amorality of party politics in a largely illiterate, tradition and caste-bound country.

Although a committed Sarvodaya (Gandhian) social worker by 1961, JP's presidential address to the 13th All-India Sarvodaya Sammelan that year made it clear that he had not renounced politics in every sense. He was explaining what the Sarvodaya disinterest in party politics meant. In view of what happened 13 years later, his speech was pregnant with warning and almost prophetic in nature. "It means, of course," he said, "that we do not belong to any political party, that we do not and shall not take part, directly, or indirectly, in any political contest for position or power. But does it also mean that we are not concerned with what is happening in the political field: with the working of our democracy and its various institutions? If democracy were to be in peril, if there was danger of political chaos, of dictatorship, shall we sit back smugly and twiddle our thumbs on the ground that we have nothing to do with politics? Perhaps it is not understood clearly that our policy not to be involved in party and power politics is meant precisely to enable us to play a more effective and constructive part in moulding the politics of the country."

II

The landscape had not changed appreciably. His thinking had. Now, approaching the age of 72, a new phase had begun. Not entirely new, for, to some extent, it involved a going back, a return to the emphasis on militancy, on resistance to a corrupt and oppressive power structure that stemmed from his Marxist years. He felt as strongly as ever about social injustice. Nothing really changed, he realized almost reluctantly, just because radical laws were passed or high-minded gestures like bhoodan made, unless continuing social or political pressures ensured that reforms were actually implemented and pledges honoured. Bihar's condition in 1974, like that of much of India, made this only too obvious. Nothing had changed in spite of the fact that, based on the pledges collected, Vinoba Bhave had been able to claim that "Bihar-dan," or a commitment by most villages in the state to the principles of bhoodan, had been achieved. He had first realized how thin the pledges were when he devoted most of 1970 to camping in an impoverished group of villages in Musahari, a subdivision of Muzaffarpur district, in an intensive effort to put up the bhoodan edifice on the foundation of the paper pledges.

In fact the disenchantment with bhoodan had begun earlier, though he had been reluctant to recognize it. The possibility that his enthusiastic conversion from party politics to bhoodan had been as much an escape as a discovery was hard to accept, especially because no third way to change society seemed available then. Even so, he had broken, now and then, out of his 20-year apprenticeship to bhoodan. But the tasks he had attempted could seldom be pursued to a conclusion (possibly they too were an escape). The outside jobs came faster towards the end of the sixties and the early seventies. They included leading a conciliation mission to Pakistan; seeking a settlement with fiercely independent Naga tribes to end the vicious circle of guerrilla insurgency and army repression; persuading traditional dacoit gangs in the Chambal ravines to give themselves up and the government to deal with them as a social rather than a criminal problem; making the world aware of the sufferings of an East Pakistan struggling to become Bangladesh.

But his disenchantment did not make him go all the way back to militant Marxism. He had become totally disillusioned with Indian communists in the pre-independence period for changing their attitude to the freedom movement as directed by the twists and turns of the Kremlin's tactical formulations based on Russia's national interest. Subsequently he had rejected Marxism itself on the ground that it provided no ethical reason to improve society. Nothing that had happened had made him change these views. But now he also remembered that Gandhi had not relied exclusively on "conversion by gentle persuasion," but also, "when the situation required," on "non-violent non-cooperation or resistance." He remained committed to the use of people's power rather than state power to achieve social change.

His militancy, too, did not imply violence. In fact, the development of his views on the fundamental issues of whether violence was necessary or justifiable in promoting change was a measure of the mental distance he had travelled since he had returned from the United States believing, like most Marxists, that violence was essential and inevitable. He had not disguised his differences with Gandhi at the time. But he had been profoundly influenced by Gandhi from the time he had begun to think about politics in school in Patna. It was in response to Gandhi's appeal to students to quit universities inculcating a slave education that he had walked out of Patna College in 1921, three weeks before he was due to sit for the examinations. It was a wrench for his parents for he was an outstanding student, normally studious and obedient. But once he had made up his mind, he could not be shaken. Since leaving college was an act of revolt against British rule, he had refused to consider going to a university in England. So he had gone to California where he had heard students could work their way through college. The Rs 2,000 wedding gift received a year earlier from the relatively affluent parents of his 14-year-old bride Prabhavati had met part of the cost of travel.

His role in the Quit India movement in 1942, when he had escaped from jail to train and direct a guerrilla sabotage campaign against the British during the Second World War, had also deviated from the methods of peaceful struggle sanctioned by Gandhi. He had carried a revolver in his belt but also issued instructions to avoid unnecessary loss of life, whether British or Indian, as by warning the authorities if a section of railway track was dynamited so that transport would be disrupted but passengers would not be killed or injured. The information did not always get through in time, however, and people were hurt. His men were armed and casualties also occurred when they clashed with the police.

This did not persuade him to stop and he continued to organize sabotage until, with a price on his head, he was recaptured in a running train in the Punjab a year later. But it did mark a big step away from the rigid, hate-inducing, black and white categories of exploiter and exploited, oppressor and oppressed, into which orthodox Marxists divided human beings, leaving no room for persuasion, change of heart, or appeals to conscience. The next stage came in 1948. Reacting against undeniable evidence of excesses committed in Stalinist Russia (which he had been reluctant to see in the thirties) and the police state that had come up in the Soviet Union in the name of Karl Marx, he publicly accepted the Gandhian politico-ethical thesis that means inevitably influenced ends and that a just society could be achieved only by using just means.

Nevertheless, he had not, and still did not, commit himself to complete non-violence. He laid stress on peaceful means, with the implication that if peaceful demonstrators were provoked by violence to react violently, the movement need not be called off—as Gandhi had done in 1922 when 22 policemen were killed by a mob in a remote UP village, Chauri Chaura. He had also consistently refused to condemn those like the Naxalites committing violence if mistakenly, for justifiable ends. He remembered that Gandhi had preferred violence to cowardice. But he advised them that violence would not work for tactical as well as moral reasons. The Indian situation could not be compared either to that of Russia or China. It had been Gandhi's genius to evolve techniques of non-violent resistance that made it possible for the bulk of the people to participate in mass struggle, to rid themselves of fear. Reliance on arms would lead to an elitist rather than a truly democratic people's movement.

III

He was not too certain about when he had last visited any particular village or travelled a road the first time. He barely noticed the lush monsoon landscape, a chequer-board of shades of green, with the delicate, almost yellow tint of the paddy predominant, rippling in the slightest breeze like wind-swept hair. He did not respond to music or the arts. He was a true intellectual with a mind that was at once analytical and architectonic. His memory was not as good as it used to be, but even now he was busily ranging over the interrelations between the political, economic, educational, and financial facets of the movement he was guiding. His writings, in precise, unambiguous Hindi and English, filled volumes. At the same time he could be sentimental about human beings, concerned about them as individuals, a trait viewed as weakness by many who had been his political colleagues. It kept him from taking the firm, decisive measures required to maintain discipline and make hard political decisions. It also led him to trust the professions of persons and groups, against the advice of his colleagues that there was risk of being betrayed, as he was repeatedly by Moscow-directed communists who were out to infiltrate and weaken the CSP. But possibly it was this that made him question the claims of any system or ideology to promote human well-being when it became too dogmatic and inflexible. For him the touchstone was the freedom of the individual, freedom from authoritarian, economic, political, bureaucratic, or traditional pressures. He had learned that a long-held ideology or system could become a substitute for religion, a shield against personal doubts and fears, a device to avoid the responsibility of individual judgment and choice.

Much of the past had become a blur punctuated by recollections of friends and comrades, many of whom were dead. But everyone knew him, of that the crowds left no doubt. He was easily recognized. Tall and spare, he had not put on weight over the years. His bearing had not slackened with age. Nor had his features lost their chiselled edge. His eyes were alert behind semi-hornrimmed spectacles, though occasionally they gave the impression that he was not giving all his attention to his immediate surroundings. His mouth was firm, with the lower lip protruding a little more than before and exaggerated even more by cartoonists seeking an easily identifiable feature. He spoke gently and with consideration for others. It was transparent sincerity, not passion, that left an impress. His hair was thinning, but there was enough for him to run a comb through before addressing a public gathering—a touch of vanity recalling the handsome, imposing young man who was always correctly dressed, whether in a sober suit abroad or a freshly-starched khadi kurta and dhoti or pyjama at home. Now he was wearing a freshly-laundered kurta and pyjama, but they were not as spotless and carefully ironed as when Prabhavati was alive.

Students felt at home with his modern idiom and revolutionary past. The years spent with Vinoba Bhave added a different but perhaps even more valuable facet to his popular image. He had shown that he could live simply, in the remotest village, like the sages that traditional India (even the caustic students) revered. He did not make a show of poverty, as Gandhi did. He travelled first class by train when the doctors advised it. But even so, his simplicity stood out in sharp relief against the air-conditioned comforts surrounding Congress leaders.

He attracted especially the young and the elderly. The middle-aged seemed reluctant to upset the *status quo*. The elderly hung back, uncertain. They had given up hope long ago, but this glimpse of a familiar figure returning to a role that recalled a more innocent, optimistic time, rekindled hope. Perhaps even now things could change. An old man in a dirty, patched-up loin cloth, skin burnt black, grizzled grey stubble on head and chin—the archetypal Indian peasant—came tentatively forward at a roadside stop joining his palms in a *namaste*. For some time he stood unnoticed but evoked a return namaste before the car moved on. Only his rheumy eyes responded with silent appeal. (Some minutes later JP remarked, half to himself: "How can anyone fulfil such expectation?") As for the students, they had not responded so enthusiastically even to Gandhi. This was their movement; they had begun it, he had joined them and continued to consult them at every step.

So they built welcome arches quickly made up of bamboo and paper over the roads, if they knew in advance which way and when he was coming. If they recognized his car in time—it was a different one for every stage of his journey for he depended on ocal friends and admirers to transport him to the next stop—they leaped and ran beside it, thrusting flowers at him, pleading with him to stop and say a few words. Sometimes, the impatience was uppermost and bouquets were hurled at him like missiles. They were merciless in their enthusiasm, shouting

"Loknayak Jayaprakash zindabad." (Long live people's hero, Jayaprakash) and other slogans into his ears until he was deafened, insisting on garlanding him until his neck was sore. The previous day he had got down to receive their greetings and was so exhausted by the evening that a doctor was called to make sure that he had not suffered a relapse. It was just two months since he had returned from hospital following a prostate operation. And his heart had given trouble too. He felt so tired occasionally that he wondered if he could go on.

So now he sometimes drove on if the students were late in recognizing him. Even if they did he refused to get down, accepting the garlands and flowers in the car till the floor and seats were covered. Flowers, especially the blood-red hibiscus, were plentiful during the monsoon, but they wilted fast. By the time he reached the day's destination, they were grey and limp. But more were always being offered.

IV

The students he saw were different from those he remembered when he was in school and college. The plain white dhoti and kurta had been abandoned. Bush-shirts in bright shades and drainpipe trousers were the current uniform. Most of them came from homes that had not changed so much. But they no longer fitted into the traditional pattern of family life in which the elders had the last word. Nor were they at home with the Westernized style they tried to adopt. It was still foreign. They had picked it up from films, picture magazines, advertisements, and by aping the more sophisticated among them. The education they got was essentially the same as he got before he went to America. It was still designed primarily to produce clerks for government offices, although the numbers passing out now were a hundred times as many as the jobs available; with a few exclusive institutions to turn out a limited number of privileged, culturally alienated, English-speaking elite that made up the new class that managed the country, its armed forces, and the bigger business and commercial concerns.

Standards had fallen. The number of students had multiplied without a comparable increase in teachers or facilities. Bihar's schools and universities were among the worst in the country. Appointments, contracts, selection of textbooks were all areas of political patronage. Cheating in examinations was customary —in the two years in which a tough civil servant acted as vice-chancellor of its leading universities, the number who passed fell below 25 per cent.

The students were aware of all this. Those who had not become cynical were angry and frustrated and no longer willing to accept parental fatalism. Certainly they were volatile and selfless enough to be agents of change. Unlike party politicians, they were more than willing to act without first calculating the profit to themselves. But could they be guided, especially by someone of so different a generation? Or would they explode into meaningless violence on a bigger scale than before—burning buses, stoning trains, attacking every symbol of the administration?

It was an old combination--a lone, aged leader with lieutenants and followers young enough to be his grandchildren. Sometimes he could hardly stand the strain. "You only know how to shout slogans," he scolded them angrily more than once. Occasionally they were so upset by his upbraiding them for lack of disclipine, or by his refusal to stop by the roadside to address them, that shouts of "Long live Jayaprakash," turned to "Death to Jayaprakash." But they had no one else to turn to, and he could find no substitute for them. When he did get a chance to talk to them at length, he enjoyed it and they listened. Even when addressing huge crowds, he was more teacher than orator. He told his audience not to waste time applauding what he said, or breaking into slogans, as the younger ones were apt to do. There was so much to learn about why the democratic system in the country, especially in Bihar, was not working to the benefit of the people, and what they could and should do about it. Often he spoke for two hours or more, pleading with those getting restive to hear him out—ignoring the monsoon rain and getting his audience and himself drenched—for they must understand, otherwise chaotic violence followed by a bureaucratic-military dictatorship was inevitable.

And that, he would point out—for it was beginning to seem to some to be the only way out—had done no good to the countries that had tried it. A glaring example was Pakistan, which the stupidity and insensitiveness of its military rulers had split into two. The Soviet experiment had ended in dictatorship by bureaucrats. The Chinese experiment was still evolving. But whatever was achieved it could not be democracy because Mao believed in the power of the gun and the bulk of the people could never have guns.

It was not hard to establish how badly things were going at home. Everyone in the audience had been affected by a price rise of more than twenty-five per cent in one year. Prices were still rising. And everyone knew that to get anything done by the government, which had involved itself at one stage or other in every civic or commercial activity, needed many palms to be greased. That it was no use complaining to a legislator or minister because he took his cut, either directly or in the name of the party, was equally evident. In Bihar they had voted out the Congress, only to find other parties equally venal—they too required money and patronage to survive in a system in which there were no effective checks against money being used to corrupt the electoral process. Those who contributed money had always to be compensated.

Bihar had been the biggest victim of such corruption. Its per capita income had fallen below even the low national average. It was one of the poorest states in the country, with two-thirds of its 60 million people subsisting below the poverty line—which meant they never had enough to eat. It had fertile soil, with perennial rivers available for irrigation. Eighty per cent of the population lived on farming. Even so the state actually imported rice and wheat. It was rich in minerals too, with plenty of coal and iron ore. Steel mills had come up, but the benefits had not trickled down to the people. Two inquiry commissions headed by retired judges of the Supreme Court had found ministers and officials responsible for corruption and nepotism on a wide scale—to no effect, even the guilty had not been punished, and were still in politics or service if they had not retired on their riches. It was a vicious circle from which there was no exit unless a new element, outside party politics, could make people realize that they had the power, and the right, to secure cleaner government.

He asked the students to be the new element, to quit their so-called studies for a year and form action committees in every high school and college. Apart from demonstrating against known hoarders and corrupt officials, their immediate objective should be to arouse public opinion against ministers, and the corrupt or incompetent legislators who kept them in office, so that they would be forced to resign. Then, together with similar non-party committees set up by their elders, to screen candidates for the next election, whether party or non-party, supporting those known to be honest. That had become a far more important qualification for office than any manifesto.

Some of the fractured Opposition parties were supporting the campaign. He met their local leaders wherever he went. Some had been his colleagues in the Socialist Party. They were as disgusted with the system as he, but had given their lives to it and had come to yearn for office and the status and influence that it could bring. His non-party approach seemed too impractical to work, at least in their lifetime. The right-wing Jana Sangh was also supporting him because of the embarrassment he was causing to the Congress, not only in Bihar but in New Delhi. Without the support of Prime Minister Indira Gandhi the Bihar ministry could not survive, as the Chief Minister himself admitted. And, on the national level, her survival also depended on the money and patronage that kept the system going.

V

Neither JP nor Mrs Gandhi was keen on a confrontation. Yet it was inevitable, for they were sustained by and represented contrary values and processes in society. He was a total, uncompromising democrat, with faith in the ability of ordinary people to find their own solutions, throw up their own leaders, and use modern technology to their own advantage if permitted to do so by a government that did not dominate and exploit them. Reacting against his early belief in state power, he had come to distrust centralized authority because it had inevitably led to domination by an elite group that used the administration and the economy to keep itself in power and comfort. He now evaluated the degree of democracy in a society by the autonomy, self-reliance, and representative nature of the smallest units at the village or municipal level rather than the functioning of a national parliament. The object of his revolution was to change society, change human values, not to overturn government—unless they stood in the way. But it was this that the country's intellectuals, brought up to think only in terms of power, in government *for* rather than *by* the people, could not comprehend, in spite of Gandhi.

Her power rested squarely on the unstated and often unconscious desire of the administrative, military, political, and business elite, who had stepped into the shoes of the British rulers and done very well for themselves over a quarter century, to extend their grip and increase their privileges. They saw the country's future in their own image and had learnt to manipulate and corrupt the electoral system to their advantage. Contrary to Gandhi's teachings, they identified nationalism with a strong, centrally-dominated state on the imperial or colonial pattern. It was only in the last few years, when the corruption and inefficiency of the administration had become too obvious, and the disparity between rich and poor too wide to be ignored that a few had begun to question their role. But as the crisis heightened, even they revealed their unconscious interests by urging the administration to acquire ever-increasing powers to deal with problems that had been created or magnified by its own corruption and incompetence. Their confidence in popular institutions was skin-deep. Populist slogans were used with the utmost cynicism to retain power.

JP and Indira Gandhi appealed to contradictory values in society as well as in each individual—the ethical approach versus realpolitik; conscience versus pragmatism. At best they could achieve an uneasy balance, but even for that he must attain a recognizable victory. That was still uncertain. He was weak in organization, in dependable workers (he had so little to offer); the enthusiasm of students could not last indefinitely. It was a strain to guide and control the movement in Bihar; to widen it might be suicidal. Above all, he was aware that his time was running out. If he could make an impression on backward Bihar—which he knew so well—if its people could once demonstrate their power to make or break the system, the rest might follow.

Then there were personal, sentimental reasons. Her father had introduced him to politics; though they had differed, they had affection for each other. He had always addressed him as "*Bhai*" (brother). And during her brief and lonely married life (Jawaharlal was immersed in politics and frequently in jail), her mother, Kamala, had turned to Prabhavati for sympathy. She had never felt at home with the affluent Westernized

Nehrus and had poured her heart out to Prabhavati.

It was hard to gauge how Indira felt at the personal level. She lived in a palace world of her own. Her letters to him were still couched in affectionate terms. Once, earlier in 1974, she had appealed to him for help and support. There had been previous occasions, too, when she had sought his assistance; and as before he had responded gladly. But her idea of help was entirely personal. She did not see it in terms of support for certain policies or programmes but as help for her to remain Prime Minister, irrespective of what her government did. She seemed to identify the country's survival with her own. To begin with, she was able to evoke a sentimental response from him, but little by little he began to question her motives and doubt whether it was possible to continue to distinguish between Jawaharlal's daughter and the woman who seemed willing to approve the most devious moves and support the most corrupt persons if they gave her political strength. Recently, beneath the friendly phraseology, traces of impatience and sarcasm had become more pronounced. She obviously felt threatened and had begun to hit back in public, especially after he had spoken of her dictatorial hold on the government and the ruling party. She had retorted—a sentence that had been widely quoted—about some people being "in the habit of giving advice on a moral plane although they lived in the posh guest houses of businessmen who took care of their travel and other expenses" in a context that could only mean him—as the newspapers had inferred.

For a man whose primary appeal was his reputation for integrity, this was clearly aimed where it would hurt most. He had replied by drawing attention to an article he had written six months earlier in response to similar attacks and insinuations in the communist press (which had been feuding with him ever since he had criticized them for toeing the Moscow line in 1941, when overnight an imperialist war became a people's war with

Hitler's attack on the Soviet Union). This went back to his association with the Congress for Cultural Freedom, as honorary president of the International Congress, which he severed when the *New York Times* disclosed that the CIA had contributed to its funds. More to the point, he retorted that his public activities were financed by friends and organizations in much the same way as Gandhi and other Congress leaders who had no personal wealth supported themselves in the struggle for independence. He had also written a personal letter to her that showed how deeply wounded he was. She replied, and later said in public that she had not named him, but had not called off the public campaign. Finally the dialogue faltered when he lost confidence in her honesty.

It was communists more than Congress Party spokesmen who stepped up the campaign against him even though it meant claiming to be the truest adherents of multi-party parliamentary democracy. They depicted him as leading the forces of right reaction and fascism. Attacks by such powerful, resourceful, and unscrupulous critics made him turn even more to students in the knowledge that only the idealistic and the politically uncorrupt could be depended upon to resist them. It had come to him only a few weeks earlier that year, that perhaps the students could be the answer to his long search for a social catalyst. That was after they had demonstrated, almost accidentally, their strength in Gujarat. A protest against bad food in a college hostel had snowballed into a violent statewide campaign against political corruption that had brought down the state government and brought about the dissolution of the state legislature despite the Prime Minister's efforts to keep it going. But the students had forgotten their long-term objectives once they had won the first battle; some had been bought over, others had split, and their movement had fizzled out. But they had shown what a mass movement, inspired and organized by students, could achieve without getting involved in party politics.

So, when the students of Bihar, who had so much more to complain about, had tried to emulate Gujarat, he had both encouraged and warned them. Bihar was a far bigger state than Gujarat and its problems more deeply rooted. But they had insisted and he had agreed to guide them, provided they promised to be peaceful and accept his strategy. The movement had been countered by harsh police methods. Hundreds of students and teachers were jailed without trial. The style of repression was no different from that used by the administration when it was protecting British rule from Gandhi's campaigns. The ruling pattern had not changed. The students had not always been peaceful, but were far more orderly than in Gujarat. Some had lost heart, but many more had been strengthened by repression. The immediate outcome was unclear. Even so, there were signs that the repercussions could be far-reaching on the pattern of Gandhi's first experiment in programmed civil disobedience in the district of Bardoli in 1922.

VI

At places, the response to his presence was enthusiastic and yet orderly in a way that reawakened hope after the disorganized receptions arranged by earnest but undisciplined students. One such experience came after a particularly disorderly scene at the small, wayside railway station of Jhajha, where he detrained at night. Hundreds of students jammed the platform, making it hard for him to get down. Some of them linked arms to make a cordon round him, still he was pushed and buffeted with deafening slogans constantly shouted in his ears. An armchair was brought to take him up the steep, narrow overbridge; tilting and swaying, it was pushed and carried through the crush of admirers, up the steep steps, through a long narrow passage and down the other side. He was shaken and angry by the time he got into a waiting car (but later promised to return to talk to the students who had waited half the day to catch a glimpse of him).

Another 30 miles by bumpy road before the journey ended at midnight at Khadigram, a training centre for Gandhian workers, established 23 years earlier on a hundred acres of undulating rocky wasteland. Morning justified the exhausting trip. The centre was now an oasis of terraced fields and orchards, irrigated from large ponds in which monsoon water collected instead of coursing down and carrying the topsoil with it. The surrounding fields had benefited too. Khadigram revived confidence in what he had long believed and taught—that for the bulk of the people, not merely the Westernized elite, to benefit, development projects should be small, decentralized, aimed at improving the quality of life rather than disrupting it with huge industries and dams that increased reliance on urbanized technicians and administrators and funds from outside. Wherever such large projects had come up, they had decreased local self-reliance and made villagers more dependent on thoroughly unscrupulous politicians and the distant corruptible bureaucrats.

There was other evidence in and near Khadigram of how little relevance the well-meaning laws enacted in distant capitals really had for much of the country. The centre ran a school in which 60 boys and girls between six and sixteen lived and studied. Their parents were landless labourers, always in debt and never able to repay the money or food they had to borrow at high interest when they did not get work owing to floods or drought. The old *zamindari* (feudal) tradition required their children to work without payment, virtually as serfs, until the debts were repaid. So they looked after cows, cut grass, weeded, ploughed, and harvested fields throughout the year. It was only after the centre had made itself felt that a few parents had gained enough courage to defy tradition and the toughs hired by big landowners to enforce it, to send their children to the Khadigram school where they would be safe. It had not been easy. Only a few days earlier an angry landowner had come to insist that the school return the boy who worked his plough. How much did his father owe, he was asked. Sixty rupees was the reply. The amount was collected and repaid, and the bondage, for one family, ended—until the next bad season.

Another experience came closer to his own, and explained why so many sincere Gandhian workers had volunteered to help his movement rather than limit themselves to Vinoba Bhave's bhoodan. Eighteen years earlier, big landlords in the area had been persuaded to donate 115 acres on which landless families had been settled. A year before, however, a group of toughs had driven a tractor over their fields and demolished their huts. They insisted that the land was not owned by those who had donated it, and showed papers procured from the local revenue official to prove their case. It took eight months for the workers at the centre to establish that the papers were false. Without the non-party pressure provided by the centre, the bhoodan experiment would have ended, as it probably had elsewhere, under the pressure of the traditional landowning class abetted by a corrupt administration and legislators indebted to the rich.

A public meeting organized in a village eight miles from Khadigram was a model of discipline. The audience was seated in rows on the ground before he arrived, with a roped-off enclosure for women. They listened to him for an hour and a half, and waited till he left before crowding the road. A purse of Rs 4,300 was collected for the campaign. Khadigram's influence was evident.

But as usual he was happiest talking to students. They were volunteers attending a two-week course at the centre to spread the campaign in rural areas. They were told about the flaws in the electoral system—how, for instance, rich parties could spend as much as they wanted in a constituency because there the law did not require them to publish their accounts; what measures other countries took to limit the role of money; how laws (like the one imposing a ceiling on land holdings) were evaded; and how and when to organize protest demonstrations against hoarders and corrupt officials.

The 9th of August found him at Monghyr, where he had his first experience of setting up relief camps for the victims of a natural disaster 40 years before—after the 1934 earthquake had levelled much of the town. Half the population came out to hear him in the vast open ground within the huge fort for which Monghyr was famous; the Ganga, so broad at this time that the further shore was barely visible, made a giant horseshoe turn to make it a natural fortress. There were more urban than rural people in the crowd for a change—possibly because the government-run district bus service had been cancelled without notice. He looked at the crowd and wondered aloud, over the microphone, whether he could meet such expectations. He was old and weak from illness, he confessed, but he would work at it as long as he was able. And when the slogans of "Jayaprakash zindabad" burst out, he asked them impatiently not to interrupt him. His time was limited. He had much to tell them.

He recalled 9 August 1942, when under Gandhi's leadership the Congress launched the last countrywide campaign against British rule—the Quit India movement. Today he was asking the Congress rulers to quit their thrones, for they too had despoiled the country. This would take a long time, involve suffering, require discipline. But from what he had seen of the anger and frustration of the youth, it could be done, provided they were peaceful and organized. They would have to focus public opinion against the legislators who had not resigned already in response to the students' demand for dissolution of the assembly. Then he went into the details of organizing action committees and how they should function. They heard him to the end, though dusk had fallen, and returned home without an incident.

On the same day the Prime Minister addressed a mammoth gathering of students in New Delhi. Congress governments and parties in every state had sent contingents by special trains and more than 3,000 buses to fill the ground near Parliament House. She drove in from Parliament House escorted by 14 Youth Congress outriders on motorcycles and, again without taking names, asked the country's youth to keep away from phony revolutions and strive instead to establish the might and greatness of India. Her speech was broadcast throughout the country by All India Radio and repeated the following morning. But the impression was soon marred. In the next few days, newspapers were full of reports of the returning students elbowing other passengers off trains, raiding station stalls for food, drinking, and rioting (one was killed when the police fired to quell a riot at Bulsar station) all the way home.

VII

When he was not touring, Jayaprakash Narayan directed the campaign from the upstairs flat in a Patna building given over to an institution that his wife had established to teach women spinning and other crafts. It was difficult to approach, especially during the monsoon, when the narrow approach roads turned to slush. And after his latest heart attack, he had to be carried up the steps in a chair. Here he had been visited by political and cultural leaders from all over India and abroad. An embarrassed state government had once offered to build him a house beside the Ganga. He had refused, saying if they were willing to spend money, they could improve the slum locality ih which he lived. Little had been done, as was the fate of any part of Patna that did not house ministers and senior civil servants.

He had many visitors, some of whom he received and listened to because he found it hard to turn anyone away—Prabhavati was no longer there to screen them unobtrusively and suggest they should not overtire him. But he looked forward to discussing the long-term implications of the movement with educationists, economists, sociologists, lawyers, and others. He aspired to a total change in lifestyles and values, not just a reformed political set-up. He had set up a group to suggest improvements in the electoral law. Now he was taking particular interest in education, trying to use the hiatus caused by his call to students to quit their studies for a year to shake the system out of its classroom, textbook, and examination-centred mould into something more suited to the country, more in tune with the latest developments abroad. He followed these developments with interest, especially the revolt against the conventional approach led by Ivan Illich and others.

Yet, when his visitors and his two devoted but not too efficient secretaries left, he was very much alone. He had no one with whom he could share his thoughts. No deputy of adequate stature, no politbureau that would not be diffident in discussing tactics with him, not even someone to take his mind off what he was doing. None of his age was of the same mental calibre; they agreed with him because they admired him. The young stimulated him occasionally, but the chasm of age could not be bridged easily.

The years had developed the teacher more than the political leader in him. The crowds that gathered to hear and see him now were not attracted by a charisma. He could be dull and long-winded at times. Nor was he a good judge of men; he took them on trust too easily. But he was learning to make essential tactical compromises. He cultivated the support of Opposition political parties, though this meant minimizing social and economic objectives on which they could disagree. He quoted Gandhi's maxim that to know the next step was enough to counter the tendency of politicians and intellectuals to sit back and pick holes in any programme put before them. He also believed that if the right conditions were created through militancy and stress on values, the rest could be left to work out itself. He had faith in the evolutionary process, provided it was not choked by executive authority. But as a tactical move he allowed the ideal of partyless democracy to appear as remote as the "withering away of the State" envisaged in communist dogma. This was a defensive reaction to Congress and communist critics who used the thesis to discredit him as a utopian, or a secret fascist. But he still had not learnt to watch his words carefully when making a public speech. Some of his phrases, especially when quoted out of context, were used against him.

Money was a difficult issue. As he had pointed out in his reply to the Prime Minister, it was nothing new for national leaders to accept the help and hospitality of affluent men when necessary. Indian and foreign philanthropists had sent him millions of rupees over the years for the many relief campaigns he had organized. But now that events had placed him in a stance of opposition to the ruling party and its leader Indira Gandhi, money or assistance accepted by him was given a political colouring. How was it any different, his critics argued, for JP to accept money from people who may have earned it illegally, or who could be corrupt? Yet the central thrust of his campaign was against corruption in political life. This was not a charge that was easy to answer. Still, without money and other forms of assistance, he could not possibly direct the movement. It would either become chaotic or be taken over by political parties. More and more came from the gatherings he addressed or the groups who collected by the wayside to thrust little cloth purses containing bundles of notes into his hands. Even so, the demands of the movement, even to provide food and shelter to the increasing number of students and other volunteers kept mounting. The real issue was how the money was used, not where it came from, provided there were no strings. About this his conscience was clear. He could not afford to delay or hold back. He had so little time to guide it until it could take off without him.

Time and momentum had become a crucial consideration, leading him not only to accept as an ally anyone willing to go along with him, but occasionally to sanction tactics without working out all the implications. At 72, and with a heart condition, his hurry was understandable. But the concern with his health began to fade as the movement gathered momentum and bigger and bigger crowds responded to his presence. He seemed to draw strength and energy from the challenge. The lassitude, pessimism, and self-doubting that had seized him after Prabhavati's death disappeared. In some ways, in fact, he showed more self-confidence than he ever had. He still listened attentively to others' opinions, but the tentativeness with which he had put forward his own, the ease with which he had been impressed by a strong personality, or moved by an appeal to sentiment was no longer evident. It was a transformation that gardually made up for the qualities he still lacked when compared to Gandhi—a charisma, political flair, skill in building a team. Nor indeed did he have such a simply expressed and comprehended goal as independence to motivate people.

But attitudes had begun to change. Even the Westernized urban intellectual who had regarded Gandhi as a crankish revivalist who would lead the country backwards, was beginning to read through his works again for a way out of the mess that uncritical acceptance of Western (including Soviet) concepts of progress through an elite-dominated industrialized economy had landed the country in. This was part of the reason that they were turning to him. But would they be willing to give up the status and privileges that the system had provided in a country of poverty-stricken villages?

The process would obviously take long. But it could not have been accelerated. Revolutions took their own time to mature, he believed; they could not be created, but could perhaps be guided when the moment was ripe. And his instinct told him that this was the moment. In fact, his life seemed a preparation for this time. Without widespread and acute economic distress and complete loss of faith in government, so many would not have been drawn to him. His simple, straightforward painstaking desire to teach and not to command, now stood out in his favour. He was an intellectual who did not belong to the remote uncaring elite. He could be trusted at a time when people had lost confidence in party leaders with their big election promises and a bureaucracy that was still colonial in style. Perhaps it had even been necessary for Prabhavati to die a year previously to impel him to plunge into so big an experiment.

In spite of the different political labels he had worn, his underlying concern for freedom and liberty had been consistent. It was in this quest that he had been attracted to one political thesis after another, and rejected them when he found that in the name of promoting freedom, they placed constraints on it. For him freedom was a comprehensive concept involved in every aspect of an individual's life in society—his schooling, social contacts, occupation, needs and ambitions. Association with Gandhi had infused his concept of freedom with an ethical flavour. Without it, he had come to realize quite early, man could be no more than a pawn in the grip of blind economic or political forces. Only the desire to do good distinguished man from brute and provided the incentive to do better. For the same reason, he rejected the economic thesis of ever-expanding wants, thus teaching, though not as strictly as Gandhi, the need for moderation and self-discipline. This was not a philosophy designed exclusively for India. He had come to it after close study of Western and Marxist values which shared the self-defeating motivation of mounting material wants.

It was after a three-week self-purificatory fast in Poona in 1952 that he had faced up fully to the unfashionable, non-Marxist concept of goodness in words that would become even more relevant in the future:

> ...the problem of human goodness is of supreme moment today. The individual asks today why he should be good. There is no god, no soul, no morality, no life hereafter, no cycle of birth and death. He is merely an organization of matter, fortuitiously brought into being and destined soon to dissolve into the infinite ocean of matter He sees all round him evil succeed—corruption, profiteering, lying, deception, cruelty, power politics, violence. He asks naturally why he should be virtuous. Our social forms of today and the materialist philosophy which rules the affairs of men answer back: he need not. The cleverer he is, the more gifted, the more courageously he practices the new amorality; and in the coils of this amorality the dreams and aspirations of mankind become warped and twisted.
>
> For many years I have worshipped at the shrine of the goddess Dialectical Materialism which seemed to me intellectually more satisfying than any other philosophy. But while the main quest of philosophy remains unsatisfied, it has become patent to me that materialism of any sort robs man of the means to become truly human. In a material civilization man has no rational incentive to be good.

He was at his best with small groups of students—a Socrates-like figure, teaching them to question the conventional and honour only the valuable. He would not lead a revolution to victory, but he could inspire it, long after he had gone. Indeed, the question of victory did not arise; it was a process he was starting, which, like learning, could never be completed.

CHAPTER TWO
EARLY YEARS

NOTHING IN the environment in which Jayaprakash Narayan was born or spent his early childhood provides a clue to the concerns that dominated his life. His father, Harsu Dayal, was a mildmannered revenue official in Bihar's canal department; his grandfather, Devkinandan Lal, a rather irascible village *darogha* (head constable). His father sympathized with the modest Congress demand for a greater degree of self-rule for India but was unable to comprehend Gandhi's tactics or objectives when he returned to India from South Africa. His mother was orthodox and the only one in the family who was regular about religious prayers and ceremonials. The home itself, which kept moving because Harsu Dayal's job transferred him from place to place, was a usual Hindu middle class establishment with few comforts. But since the family was of the enlightened Kayastha caste, there were plenty of books and magazines and they kept in touch with events by subscribing to the *Amrita Bazar Patrika*, a Calcutta newspaper.

The burning nationalism that made JP respond to Mahatma Gandhi's call to quit college and inspired him to organize a guerrilla force in 1942 and resist torture on his recapture, cannot be traced to family influence. Nor did he resent the family's limited world which fitted into the traditional caste matrix. He was no young rebel. Studious and somewhat withdrawn, he did whatever his parents or elder relations wanted. As a child he was nicknamed "Baul"—innocent to the point of being a simpleton. While he was clearly in advance of his age in intelligence, his lack of guile, ready trust in others and complete absence of personal aggrandizement meant that he could be easily exploited or done out of his share. But he did not seem to mind or even notice. When staying with his brother-in-law, Braj Behari Sahai, as a student in Patna, he readily learnt to cook for the family when they were unable to get a Brahman cook. According to the strict caste conventions by which they lived, they could take food only from one of the family if a Brahman cook was not available.

JP was born soon after the turn of the century, on 11 October, 1902, in the family home at Sitabdiara village on the confluence of the Ganga and Ghagra rivers on Bihar's border with what was then the United Provinces and is now Uttar Pradesh. Neither the house nor the village remains where it was. The site was gradually eroded by the shifting rivers and Sitabdiara was rebuilt on the other bank. Some of the original beams of the house were rescued by JP and became part of the new house he built in the adjoining Ballia district of UP. The shifting rivers had made him a resident of UP instead of Bihar.

In effect, Jayaprakash was the eldest son. An older brother and sister had died at an early age of cholera. He had two more sisters, Chandrakala and Chandravati, one older and one just younger, and a brother, Rajeshwar, born eight years after him, to whom he was as indulgent as a fond uncle. Rajeshwar was somewhat spoilt and very ill-tempered. There were occasions when he turned on his elder brother, hitting and kicking him but he does not recall JP ever losing his temper; he merely held him at a distance and calmed him down.

JP was a serious child burdened with an early sense of responsibility due to the tragic death of the eldest brother. He did not play very much with toys or other children, but was fond of birds and animals. In a note written in 1963, his sister Chandrakala recalled his father giving him a pair of pigeons. One became sick and died in spite of his careful nursing. He was unable to eat or sleep that day. This sensitivity to suffering never left him. Some 60 years later, during his campaign to relieve the suffering from the great drought that hit Bihar in

Early Years

1966-67, his associates recall that he was unable to eat if he saw a death from starvation and had to take sleeping pills for some days. Even as a child he was concerned about adult suffering. When his father wanted to dismiss an incompetent tutor, JP insisted that he be kept on.

Most of his time was spent reading. By the age of ten, he was reading historical novels glorifying the kings and heroes of ancient India. He soon graduated to the works of Bankim Chandra Chatterjee that had been recently translated from Bengali into Hindi. He also read about foreign national heroes like Garibaldi and de Valera. All this aroused his first feeling of nationalism, but it was more historical and literary than related to the country's current condition.

His first exposure to the wave of nationalist feeling inspired by Gandhi came soon after he was sent to Patna to enter the Patna College School at the age of 11 or 12. For a while he stayed with a relative, Shambu Sharan Verma, and then in a students' hostel—Saraswati Bhawan—in which most of the boys were quite a bit older. Among them were some of Bihar's future leaders: its first Chief Minister, Srikrishna Sinha, his second-in-command, Anugraha Narayan Sinha, Ram Charita Singh, another minister, and several others who were to become widely known in politics and the academic world.

Gandhi had not returned from South Africa, but the magic word "satyagraha" had become known in India after his protracted civil resistance campaign in the Transvaal succeeded after nearly six years in securing the repeal of blatantly racist legislation. The hated poll tax on indentured Indian labour was removed and the South African government committed itself to abolish the system of importing indentured labour from India by 1920. All this had been achieved peacefully by the willingness of a few thousand Indian immigrants in South Africa to go to jail rather than accept unjust laws. That was in a foreign country. What could satyagraha not achieve at home? All at once, independence seemed attainable and every student felt that he could participate in the struggle—not leave it to lawyer-politicians or isolated revolutionaries.

But was satyagraha merely a technique for a backward, unarmed people, or did it imply a commitment to non-violence? The call of the revolutionary and the terrorist, for which neighbouring Bengal was known, was also attractive, more so for students. Although interest in satyagraha mounted with Gandhi's return to India in 1915, and he began to be called "Mahatma," the lure of violent revolution did not flag. JP was still in school in his early teens when a companion, Chotan Singh, introduced him to a youthful revolutionary from Bengal. They met in secret on a deserted stretch beside the Ganga. The revolutionary told him about terrorist exploits in Bengal and gave him some pamphlets as well as a book proscribed by the government, *Desh ki baat* (facts about our country), that described how the British were exploiting India. He told him what dangerous lives they led and the tests initiates had to take to prove their loyalty. JP was impressed by the initiation rite—holding a finger in a candle flame without flinching—and found himself attracted by dreams of reviving the country's historic glory (which he remembered from books read at home). They met several times, but one day the revolutionary disappeared. And soon the police arrested Chotan Singh. Many years later he could recall how they tied his hands with rope, in spite of his youth, and marched him to the police station.

But JP did not allow all this to affect his studies. By now he was an outstanding student. He read widely, was fascinated by English literature and learnt to write well in the language. Many of his friends were reading law and they spoke to one another in English. But he did not forsake Hindi, as some did. He experimented in writing plays and even some poetry. An essay he wrote in a Hindi competition on "The State of Hindi

Early Years

in Bihar" won the prize, even though college students had also competed for it.

The only blot on his school career was the occasion when he boycotted classes because they were held on the day of Raksha Bandhan. The headmaster, Whitmore, an Englishman, called for him and told him that though he was a good student and he (Whitmore) liked him, it was his duty to punish him. JP got five strokes with the cane but far from becoming embittered, found he rather admired his headmaster for doing his unpleasant duty.

The mathematics teacher also left a profound impression by his devotion to his students. He awakened JP's interest in the subject, which served him well later. English was taught by a Muslim teacher, who encouraged him to read literature and poetry. Through him he discovered Shakespeare, Keats, Shelley and the romantic poets. His old-world courtesy also gave young JP an early glimpse of the rich Urdu culture that had survived the Mughal court.

At about this time, his local guardian was his brother-in-law, Braj Behari Sahai, who had got to know one of the most brilliant barristers in Bihar, Rajendra Prasad, future President of India. And it was at Rajen Babu's house that JP, now nearly 18, was introduced to another outstanding barrister, Braj Kishore. Both were Congressmen—as many lawyers were—and had already made a reputation in law and in political life that extended beyond the province.

Both lived well, but had been influenced by Gandhi. The first time Gandhi saw Braj Kishore at the Lucknow Congress session in 1916 he was not greatly impressed, as he recalled later in his *Autobiography:* "He was dressed in a black alpaca achkan and trousers. Brajkishore Babu failed then to make an impression on me. I took it that he must be some vakil (lawyer) exploiting the simple agriculturists." But Gandhi was considerably impressed later, when Braj Kishore gave up his thriving practice (he had been staggered by the fees barristers charged. Rs 10,000 was not unusual for a case) to join him in collecting evidence of the cruel exploitation of indigo workers in the Bihar district of Champaran, a name that was to become famous as the scene of Gandhi's first success in India, much of it the result of Braj Kishore's help.

It was not much more than three years later that Braj Kishore saw JP and was so impressed by him that he promptly arranged a match with his younger daughter, Prabhavati. (His elder daughter had married his good friend and colleague Rajen Babu's son Mrityunjaya.) They were soon married though Prabhavati was only 14. This was not unusual; it was a customary formality. The young couple did not live together. After the ceremony the bride returned to her parental home. But JP had married into one of the best known families in Bihar—a marriage that would deeply influence his personal and political life in unexpected ways.

By now he had also passed his matriculation examination in the first division, doing well enough to get a government scholarship of Rs 15 a month. He had no trouble gaining admission to the intermediate science classes in Patna College. Everything seemed set for a brilliant academic career, though not in law; the young Jayaprakash preferred chemistry and mathematics.

Heated political discussions convulsed the student community, for these were eventful days. The war had ended but the wartime restrictions on free speech, the press, the right of assembly, were extended and made statutory by the infamous Rowlatt Act. Even worse was to follow: the Jallianwala Bagh massacre took place on 13 April 1919, setting the country aflame. Gandhi went from district to district and finally began his first countrywide non-cooperation movement in 1920 when JP had his first glimpse of him addressing a public meeting. Though exciting, these events did not initially disturb the tenor of JP's studious life. His guardian disapproved of cinemas, even games. Every day JP returned from his classes to study at home. Nothing outside had really threatened to disturb his daily routine after the Bengali revolutionary disappeared.

Then, one day, less than a month before his I.Sc examination was due to begin, Maulana Abdul Kalam Azad and Jawaharlal Nehru addressed a public meeting in Patna. Although only 33 at the time, Azad was already known throughout the country for his learning and his command over the Urdu language. As a Muslim intellectual who had broken away from orthodoxy and embraced the nationalist cause, he was also something of a rarity, especially in Bengal, where, for historical reasons, the revolutionary movement was almost entirely Hindu. The students of Patna discovered that the young, handsome Maulana was an even more powerful orator than a writer. In fact, he overshadowed the younger Jawaharlal. And coming from him, a widely-travelled and sophisticated Muslim from Calcutta, Gandhi's appeal to students to leave schools and colleges that were financed by a foreign government and imparted an education, designed to produce clerks for the British administration proved more convincing than all that they had read or discussed so far. Years later, when he was asking students to leave their colleges and join the movement he was guiding, JP could still recall the elegant couplet in Urdu that was Azad's reply to those who argued that until Gandhi established more suitable colleges and schools, there was no alternative to studying in the existing ones: "Must a man tasting poison wait till nectar is available before he stops taking it?"

Almost all the leading students in Patna College resolved to quit their classes from that day. "I was one of the thousands of young men of those days," he recalled later, "who, like leaves in a storm, were swept away and momentarily lifted up to the skies. That brief experience of soaring up with the winds of a great idea left imprints on the inner being, that time and much familiarity with the ugliness of reality have not removed."

JP wrote to his father who wanted him at least to take the final examination before leaving Patna College. But the quiet, obedient student was adamant. He took to weaving khadi and learnt to spin on the charkha. He was finally persuaded to take the exam from the Bihar Vidyapeeth which had just been established for students who had left aided colleges, and passed with distinction. But the Vidyapeeth could only provide instruction up to the intermediate standard. He refused to join Banaras Hindu University which provided a more Indian style of education because it received a grant from the government, and its founder, Pandit Madan Mohan Malaviya, had opposed Gandhi's call to students to leave colleges.

His father, and even more his father-in-law Braj Kishore, felt they could not allow such a brilliant student to end his education so precipitately. When study in the country was ruled out, they thought of England where so many eminent Indians, like Jawaharlal Nehru, had studied. But JP would not agree. It seemed absurd to his logical mind to refuse to study at an Indian university because it was financed and influenced by the imperial government, but be willing to study in the country that ruled and exploited India. Money was another problem. His family was too poor to maintain him abroad for long. Having given up his practice to work for the Congress, his father-in-law was no longer as affluent as before. So money was a major consideration. This led him to think of America, specifically California, where quite a number of Indians had worked their way through college. The successful American War of Independence against the British was another attraction for JP.

He went to Calcutta to be fitted out in Western clothes for the first time, at the age of 19. This was his first glimpse of a big city. Later, the urbanized socialists of Bombay could not refrain from expressing their surprise—and exhibiting their own sophistication—by noting that this was the first time that JP saw a tram-car. (In course of time he would provide an essential link between them and the more indigenous socialists in eastern India.) With the Rs 2,000 gift received from Braj Kishore in his marriage, and contributions from both families, enough money was collected to pay his fare and start him off with $600 in cash. There was a moment of last-minute hesitation when reports were received that work had become hard to get in the United States. But another student, Bholadutt Pant, had preceded him and wrote back to say things were not so bad. However, Prabhavati refused to accompany him. Soon after their marriage, she had been sent by her father to stay with Gandhi at Sabarmati, where she became fully involved in the rigorous life of the ashram. Besides, he knew that her husband would find it difficult to support both of them.

So in 1922, as the monsoon was breaking, JP embarked on the *Janus* at Calcutta for Kobe. It was not too pleasant a voyage. The sea was rough and he was seasick. It was a cargo boat that carried a few passengers. JP was too shy to make friends easily with foreigners and his vegetarian diet meant eating in his cabin. But two young Indian cabin-mates, Sitaram Reddy and Harishchandra Pradhan, kept him from getting too lonely. The *Janus* called at Rangoon, Penang, Singapore and Hong Kong *en route* to Kobe and they made the most of each stop. Each place had the glamour of a foreign city, but JP also noticed how much in common they had with conditions in his own country. The most memorable part of the voyage was a frightening passage through the tail of a typhoon in the South China Sea in which there were moments when it seemed certain that the ship would sink.

After such a voyage, it was a relief when the ship docked at Kobe. JP was entranced by the delicate beauty of the Japanese countryside and was even more impressed by the courtesy, cleanliness and efficiency of the people. He spent nearly a month in the country, staying at inexpensive Japanese-style hotels and, fresh from India, was relieved to find that tradition and efficiency could be combined. He worked as proof-reader on the *Mainichi* to earn some money. Finally, at Yokohama, he took a Japanese liner, the *Tayo Maru* to San Francisco. Two young Bengalis joined the three from India there. Thanks to them, the group became more sociable, chatted to other passengers and played cards during the 18-day voyage. But JP remained withdrawn compared to the others. On 8 October 1922 the ship sailed into San Francisco harbour, one of the most scenic natural anchorages in the world—an impressive entrance to the United States.

CHAPTER THREE

AMERICA AND MARXISM

NO ARRANGEMENTS had been made for JP or his fellow passengers to be received in San Francisco. But entry into the United States was far less complicated in the early twenties, and the young group did not feel too strange once there. San Francisco has known many Chinese and Indians. It was the port of entry for Asians, though not on the scale that New York, on the east coast, attracted Europeans. Many members of the Ghadar (north Indian revolutionary) Party who had been externed from India had settled in California. JP contacted one of them who advised the group to stay in the Nalanda Club, an inexpensive hostel for Hindus (as all Indians were called to distinguish them from Red Indians) at Berkeley.

After spending the night at a cheap hotel for negroes, the group crossed the Bay by boat to Berkeley (the Oakland Bay bridge had not yet been built) to seek admission in the University of California. JP was charmed by the beautiful setting of the sprawling campus on a range of hills rising out the ocean. But the first term had started. Neither he nor his friends had enough money to wait for the next semester in January without getting jobs. But there were enough Indians in Berkeley to advise them on how to get work.

After a few days at the Nalanda Club, JP and Sitaram Reddy, one of the students who sailed with him from Calcutta, set out for nearby Marysville. There they met Sher Khan, a Pathan overseer, a huge bear of a man who had been externed from India. More than 50 years later JP recalled the affection and regard with which he received them. "I should kiss your feet," he had said, "because you have just come from India." He directed them to a grape orchard which paid 40 cents an hour for working a nine-hour day. The gang that they joined was composed entirely of Pathans, but in deference to the sentiment of the new arrivals, no beef was eaten. The newcomers were very popular. The older residents were eager to know what was happening at home. They had heard of Gandhi and were most impressed that JP had left college in response to his call.

JP and Reddy shared a hut in which the only furniture was two wooden bunks covered with straw on which they slept. He did not find the work too hard; late autumn was mild in the spectacular north California countryside. His job was to select grapes suitable for drying as raisins. Soon he exulted in the knowledge that he could earn his keep through labour, something unheard of in his middle class Kayastha background. He was able to save almost all that he earned and when the grape-picking season ended after a month, felt rich enough to return to the Nalanda Club.

In January he was admitted into the second year, getting a year's credit for his Indian intermediate science degree. His main subjects were mathematics, chemical engineering and biology, for his initial interest lay in science. He got straight A's in all subjects, except in practicals when he found it hard to follow the American accent. In his spare time he set type for a publication providing information for Indian students. He had few other interests and was still a serious, ascetic young man. All the same he had adapted himself without stress to American conditions. Considering his traditional background, it was a surprisingly smooth transition. But Berkeley was expensive. With the $600 he had brought from home and the extra he earned on the grape orchard rapidly dwindling, he shifted to Iowa State University in Iowa city, where the fees were a quarter of Berkeley's. His pathfinder, Bholadutt Pant, was there and had found it much more economical. Even so, he had to work hard to pay his way and took whatever jobs were available in a small town—working as a waiter in a restaurant, cleaning and varnishing furniture, washing windows and shovelling snow in the depth of winter.

By now the American accent was no obstacle and he had no difficulty in keeping pace with the lecturers. But attendance was a problem, especially in winter. After working late into the night as a waiter in a restaurant or at some other job that paid by the hour, it was hard to face an icy winter morning. He could not afford the kind of clothing needed for such weather. So, he often stayed in bed late and missed the early lectures. This made no difference to his scholastic performance. He continued to get straight A's in all subjects, but was short of attendance in German. He asked his professor, a strict disciplinarian why attendance was so necessary when he had got an A in the examination and demonstrated his knowledge of the subject in seminars. But the professor insisted that joining a university implied a contract by the student to pass examinations as well as to attend classes regularly, and refused to allow him a credit for the subject.

Long after, JP called the incident evidence of the irrationality of conventional education, even in the United States, where the credit system allowed far more flexibility than in India. If a student was able to prove that he had learnt what was required in his own way, why place so much emphasis on attendance? The beginnings of his interest in a new, convention-free educational system which would encourage and provide facilities for a student to pursue knowledge in his own time and style originated in this experience, and later became a facet of the total revolution for which he campaigned.

He became known and admired on the Iowa campus for his penetrating intellect. But though he had many companions, he had few friends. Essentially, he was still a serious, single-minded young man in his early twenties and was in the United States to study. Nothing else interested him. The campus was less attractive and more conventional than Berkeley. After completing a year's study, he felt the need to move on in quest of money and a more stimulating environment. So, much of the next three years were spent in Chicago, where work was more readily available, and in the politically aware and attractive atmosphere of the University of Wisconsin at Madison. The experiences he had and the friends he made synthesized into the first sharply-defined political thesis he accepted after the vague nationalism of the college environment at Patna.

Chicago was still a boom city, though its growth was beginning to be checked by the forces that led to the Great Depression in 1929. Immigrants from Europe were flocking in, providing cheap labour for commercial and industrial enterprises. Their entry had been checked by the Great War, when thousands of negroes came in from the south to man wartime factories and stayed on to be the victims of racial violence. Corruption was a byword and the era of gang warfare had begun. In contrast to the squalid conditions in which most immigrant workers lived, parts of the city reeked with riches, mostly ill-gotten.

His stay in Chicago, on and off for three years, would leave an indelible mark on JP's personality. He worked on all kinds of jobs—shovelling snow, cleaning hotel bathrooms, turning out nuts and bolts in one factory, packaging pottery in another. To cap it all, he even worked in the city's world-famous stockyards in which great herds of cattle brought in from the western states were slaughtered to satisfy the mounting appetite of the industrialized east for meat. He found it hard to stand the sight of so much blood and got a job in the power house. On another occasion, he peddled "Himalayan herbs" made up locally with limited success. He was not a good salesman, but a handsome young Asian had curiosity value. This could be embarrassing, as he found when invited into a flat by a young maidservant who had other intentions in mind. JP had to leave hurriedly, leaving his herbs behind. In his spare time he began to read European literature and was particularly impressed by Anatole France and Henrik Ibsen. He also took lessons in Bengali from a group of Bengali students. He learnt ballroom dancing and took a liking to Greta Garbo films, but these pursuits were marginal to his other interests.

Chicago was where he became seriously ill when seeking work to finance a proposed visit to Moscow. Most places had "No Vacancy" signs on their doors; the few with jobs usually turned away negroes, Mexicans and Asians—anyone coloured. In winter, the roads were covered with snow for weeks and icy winds blowing across Lake Michigan made it torture to venture out. It was on one such day, after hours of fruitless search for work, that he found himself without the five cents needed to take the tram home. He had to walk all the way back on the ice-covered roads without an overcoat and with large holes in his shoes. He was near collapse when he got home—a room rented from an Indian couple from the West Indies. An incorrect diagnosis by a cheap doctor made things worse. He did not get up again for five months and may not have survived but for the care that the West Indian couple took of him. By this time he was $900 in debt. Far from working his way to Moscow, he had to write home for money. It was sent to him by his father, who mortgaged a part of the family's village land for the purpose.

Fortunately, the Wisconsin University campus in Madison provided a completely different environment. Laid out in the vicinity of two lakes, it had the quiet scenic beauty for which the state is known. That was not all. In the twenties, Wisconsin was one of the most liberal states in the country. This was the heritage of Robert Marion La Follette, its most outstanding politician. La Follette belonged to the Republican Party but guided its progressive wing, much in the same way as the Congress Socialist Party would attempt, unsuccessfully, to modify Congress policies. He insisted on major reforms of which the most important ended the costly privileges that the private railway interests enjoyed. Among his other contributions to Wisconsin as governor of the state, was an inheritance tax and a civil service cadre, both revolutionary concepts at the time.

When JP was in Wisconsin, La Follette had ceased to be governor and had become a progressive senator in Washington. There he pushed through a resolution demanding an investigation into the Teapot Dome scandal, one of the biggest in an era not known for democratic virtues. The hearings began in October 1923, before JP went to Madison, but remained in the headlines for almost a decade—far outdoing the Watergate scandal of more recent vintage. It was also a far worse scandal because it involved the transfer of oilfields owned by the US navy (one in Wyoming was named "Teapot Dome") to private interests, a deal from which US interior secretary Albert Fall and many other federal officials benefited. Thanks to La Follete, Wisconsin took the lead in campaigning for clean government in a permissive era. All this clearly left an indelible mark on JP. His concern with corruption as well as his confidence in public inquiries as a remedy originated in Wisconsin.

Yet it was in these liberal and attractive American surroundings that he rejected the capitalist system. For it was here that he met a brilliant young Polish Jew, Abram Landy, who was a member of the American Communist Party. And it was as a result of his friendship that he met other Marxists and began to read the communist classics as suggesting a solution to the social and political ills he found in America. He waded through all three volumes of *Das Kapital* and all the works of Engels and other early communist theoreticians that he could find. Between them, Chicago and Madison came to represent the problems of capitalism and their Marxist solution. Through Landy he met Manual Gomez, a trade union leader, and helped him organize local strikes. The communist study cell met at a small tailor's shop owned by an immigrant from Russia who

America and Marxism

laboriously read and translated Russian newspapers and ideological journals to them.

And it was Landy who introduced him to the works of M.N. Roy—closely-reasoned pamphlets that seemed to rip Gandhi's strategy of non-cooperation to shreds. As interpreted by Roy, dialectical materialism provided a more scientific analysis of India's ills and a far more historically reassuring picture of the future. Later he came upon his *India in Transition* and was even more impressed. The thought of an Indian being a colleague of Lenin, impressing his views on the Communist International and travelling from China to Mexico to inspire revolution, made him a revolutionary hero in the eyes of JP.

The overall impact, in a period in which no new positive moves towards independence were being made in India, was overwhelming. Marxism seemed to provide not only the key to independence, but to social equality and even personal liberty in those halcyon days. Lenin had just died, the harsher implications of his autocratic thesis of "democratic centralism" were little known outside Soviet borders and Stalin's excesses were yet to come. The intellectual ferment intoxicated the youthful JP and marked a milestone in his life and thinking—as significant as the impact of Maulana Azad's speech in Patna.

He became so interested in communism that Landy suggested that he go to the Soviet Union and train there to liberate his country. If he found the steamship fare himself, he was told, the party would look after him in Russia. That was what impelled him to brave the icy streets of Chicago to find work. His five-month illness ended the project. When his father sent him the money to repay his debts, he and his father-in-law advised him against visiting the Soviet Union. If he did, they warned him, the British government would not permit him to return to India.

Meanwhile, he had given up science and taken up sociology and economics in keeping with his new interest in man's evolution and the economic basis of society. When Landy found a better position as teacher at the University of Ohio, in Columbus, he accompanied him and got his B.A. degree there. For the first time, he found himself in relatively comfortable financial circumstances because he was appointed assistant professor while reading for his M.A. The brilliant young monastic Indian became a well known figure on the campus. Even after 40 years, a fellow student, Saul D. Ozer remembered clearly the impression he made when interviewed in Washington in March 1968 by Nageshwar Prasad of the Gandhian Institute of Studies, Varanasi.

Ozer recalled that while JP was never inconsiderate to his teachers or fellow-students, "I had never met a person who was more awake and intellectually alive to the implication of whatever anybody in that class said. He was always like an architect, developing his case and his argument...Narayan was never rude, but Narayan was as sharp as a knife. And Narayan followed every argument to its logical conclusion. And as a logician he was superb."

While Marx had made a strong impression on JP, Gandhi had not been forgotten. As Ozer put it: "I had a feeling that he was profoundly aware of and understood Marxism, that he had studied it, that he had absorbed it, but it was still a strange mixture of Marxism with Gandhism at that time. It was obvious that there was some conflict and he was trying to reconcile them...

"I'll tell you a very interesting discussion that I had with him. He admitted that though he was very impressed with Marxism, he was very unimpressed with communists as he found them...He told me that the major thing that bothered him was the morality, character, integrity of the communists. He found them people that he did not like. Intellectually he was trapped, but he was a man of deep ethical feeling. He was never able to give it up. He never really made the transformation to materialism."

Ozer thought that JP may not have accepted communism if he had belonged to a country with less serious problems; but "he was looking for an answer for India, which he could not see in American experience. He had to have a tremendously profound change, and that profound change he saw in communism. I was arguing from the viewpoint of America and I fought him all the time. The fact of the matter was, that whole year was a fight between Narayan and myself. In every classroom and in every waking hour. He a communist and I a Fabian socialist....With me emphasizing education and the necessity to convert people slowly and getting down to peoples, and Narayan in a big hurry, ever wanting to use the instrumentalities even of violence and action to get to the good things. The end with Narayan was always ethical, but the debate was always underneath, and I, being a product of the American scene was not in as great a hurry as Narayan who was speaking from the depth of what he had seen." Though they differed, "we all felt there was greatness in Narayan."

Even though JP was a handsome young man in his midtwenties, he retained a monastically innocent air. Ozer recalled that when they entered the library to study "it wasn't more than five minutes before every seat was filled with girls looking at Narayan...he fascinated them. The eyes of the man, the appearance of the man, was the appearance of a prophet. But I never saw him react to any of those girls...he always spoke of his wife and his regard for her and his desire to get back. I never saw him dating. I never knew that he dated, and I spent enough time with him. It would have come out."

Evidently JP was quite a puritan. The "thing he was most antagonistic to in his friends," said Ozer, "even the ones who taught him communism at Wisconsin and Chicago, was their lack of morality, their lack of care for their families, their sex morality. He mentioned that those who most influenced him intellectually most revolted him morally. And this I have a feeling came out later, but when it came to dealing with communists as individuals, as power-seekers, that strain in him, the fact that they were not moved by Gandhian purity...when I was told that he had revolted against communism my reaction was that he revolted against communists."

Ozer must have known JP well. In the interview (which took place in 1968) he commented that he had been puzzled by reports that he "was very much calmed down" because "the Narayan that I knew was a man who should have been in action. In fact that still puzzles me, how Narayan is able to stay out of politics and the political field."

None of the intelligent students of his class "would have anything but have expected Narayan, to turn out to be a great leader of India." At the same time, however, "I got the feeling of a man seeking answers, not a man seeking a way to grab power. I think that this was one of the things that revolted him with communists; his belief that they were making use of communism, that it was a means to personal power....A good number of communists believe in their own personal superiority and if only they were given power they would direct things correctly. I don't think he ever felt that way. There was no relating of this revolutionary conception to the possibility of his being the leader directing the things....Narayan was not looking as to how he could run or save India. He was trying to find out what techniques would save India."

JP's thesis for his M.A., "Social Variations," brought him considerable recognition on the campus. It examined the current theories of social change and found all of them wanting in one respect or another. It did not put forward any comprehensive new theory; it laid emphasis on the need for much more empirical study before firm conclusions could be drawn and tended to disbelieve in accidental or unique factors as responsible for social change. What won him recognition was the razor-sharp logic, lucid thinking, and wide reading the thesis displayed. What is relevant in explaining JP's own subsequent development was his acceptance of the view that the study of social change should be confined to predictable material phenomena, thus paving the way for a Marxist approach to social evolution, though Karl Marx was not mentioned in the thesis. But he was not dogmatic. He explained that only this kind of empirical approach could be useful in learning how to control or predict social change. He did not, however, rule out completely the possibility of an unpredictable factor such as genius or invention being responsible for change.

The testimonials his teachers gave him in May 1929, when he applied for a fellowship in New York, indicate the impact he had made on them. Professor F.E. Dumley of the sociology department wrote: "Intellectually, it seems to me, Mr Narayan ranks as high as or higher than any student I have ever had. He is a careful and critical thinker, and a searcher after truth, of course he is a wide reader. He is, in every sense, a scholar in the making." Professor Albert Weiss of the psychology department wrote: "In his class work on theoretical psychology I think he is one of the brightest students I have ever had.... My impression at this time is that he had in him qualifications which under favourable conditions will lead to an outstanding position as a social theorist." Professor Richard Steinmetz: "Perhaps Mr J.P. Narayan's most remarkable trait, to one living in a materialistic civilisation, is his idealism. It infuses his daily life as well as his world outlook. It has been my experience in living with him to be surprised again and again by little unexpected acts of unselfishness."

JP had just decided to go in for a Ph. D. when he heard that his mother was seriously ill. He promptly gave up his studies and spent a month in New York trying to earn enough to pay his fare to London. But the Great Depression had arrived and work was scarce. He was sitting disconsolate at the Rockefeller

Centre one day when an old acquaintance, Aurangabadkar, who had done well in America, greeted him. He had been looking for JP to accompany him on a trip to Europe and when he realized his plight, promptly offered to pay his passage to London. The local Indian student community, including his old friends Bholadutt Pant and Sitaram Reddy, gave him a farewell party at which they persuaded him to at least smoke a cigarette before leaving the shores of the United States.

At about this time, he developed his first differences with the communist line as laid down by Moscow. Lenin had urged communists to support nationalist movements in colonial countries even if they did not control them, but the latest instruction from the Comintern was that they should not only keep out of such movements but denounce them as benefiting only the bourgeoisie. This was the first of a series of disastrous and opportunistic reversals of policy that isolated the communists from the nationalist mainstream in India and other colonial countries. It was impossible for a man with JP's background and dedication to the independence of his country to swallow the new line. Upon his arrival in London, he had to wait another month for his family to raise the rest of his fare home. He spent much of it arguing the issue with English communists, but to no purpose. Like the faithful elsewhere, they were committed to the party line laid down by Moscow.

He returned to India late in 1929, after seven years abroad, still a serious, single-minded man. Except for academic and political influences, he had picked up little from his stay in America. He had sipped a drink a few times, smoked a cigarette or two, but was naturally abstemious. But he had become a Marxist—quite characteristically, he had decided that it was the latest Soviet interpretation of the Marxist theory that was mistaken, not Marxism itself. As his teachers had discovered before, he refused to accept anything just because it was handed down from authority; his own critical intellect had to be satisfied.

America and Marxism

His mother was still ailing when he got home on 23 November. She arranged for the traditional puja ceremonies held after a journey abroad. He went through them without objecting. Later, when an interviewer colleague asked how he, a confirmed Marxist, could go through such religious ceremonies, he replied that as far as possible he liked to avoid hurting people's personal sentiments. This sensitivity to the feelings of others would be criticized in future as weakness. But it was entirely consistent with his distaste for imposing even the most progressive views on anyone whose sentiments they offended.

He may not have realized it at the time, but this conviction bore the seed of his future disenchantment with Marxism, and later with any form of power politics.

CHAPTER FOUR

THE YOUNG CONGRESSMAN

WHEN JP returned to India at the age of 27, Gandhi was preparing for the next phase of the struggle for independence after a period of apparant quiescence. It was a period in which Gandhi was trying to teach his countrymen to prepare and purify themselves for freedom by learning to become self-reliant, honest and disciplined—for which khadi and the spinning wheel were symbols. He did not talk about gaining power or about the end of British rule. That would follow automatically when Indians were ready to rule themselves. With less emphasis being laid on struggle and satyagraha, those who preferred a slow constitutional/reformist approach gained strength.

The impatient younger generation regarded this preparatory phase as unduly passive, even though Gandhi came out occasionally to fight specific campaigns, such as to organize the boycott of the Simon Commission in February 1928, and the second Bardoli satyagraha which began on 28 February that year and lasted until the government repealed the 22 per cent increase in taxes that sparked the satyagraha on 6 August. JP was as much if not more impatient than the group of younger leaders of the Congress, such as Subhas Chandra Bose and, somewhat more cautiously, Jawaharlal Nehru, to begin the fight to capture power from the British. More than 40 years later, however, he would appreciate the role that Gandhi was playing—trying to build from below, encouraging grassroots organizations like village panchayats to take decisions cooperatively and independently, making them the foundations of a democratic system. What Gandhi had feared had been demonstrated only too clearly in the first 25 years of independence—that possession of state power, without the counterbalance of grassroots democracy, would not improve the plight of the average underprivileged Indian but only promote an unprincipled struggle between dominant groups for positions of power.

On returning home, he slipped back easily into the kurta and dhoti, discarding Western clothes until he visited the West again. His parents had aged considerably in his absence. His sisters were married. He was unable to recognize his brother Rajeshwar who was barely 12 when he left and was now a young man. But thanks to the photographs he had sent home from America, his family had no difficulty recognizing him even though he too had matured from an introspective student to a well-built handsome young man, reflecting the self-confidence gained by earning his own livelihood and the political assurance that Marxism gave him. But he had not become arrogant, nor did he affect a Westernized manner.

With a foreign degree and well-connected as he was through marriage with the most influential families in Bihar, well-paid jobs could have been his for the asking and he needed a steady income. He considered the possibility of opening a department of sociology in Banaras Hindu University but was eager to join the movement for independence, which meant joining the Congress. Though still an orthodox Marxist, he could see that only the Congress, led by Gandhi, had the mass following that could win independence for the country. The Communist Party, following the Comintern line at the time, not only stayed away from the freedom struggle but denounced it as representing only the interests of the bourgeoisie.

The first political gathering he attended after his return was a Congress meeting at Monghyr. The strain between the younger revolutionaries and older conservatives was now in the open, with the younger group urging the Congress to demand total independence and the conservatives willing to settle for dominion status. The changed environment was reflected in the fact that the younger group carried the day.

After seeing his parents, he went to Gandhi's ashram at Wardha. Prabhavati had lived with the Gandhis for most of the seven years he had been away; she was now 21, an attractive and intelligent young woman. Gandhi and Kasturba had treated her as a daughter and she had identified herself with them more closely than their own children. (Kasturba died in her arms while in detention in the Agha Khan's palace in Poona in 1944.) Inevitably, she had come to accept Gandhi's views on the need for women to play their part in the country's social and political advancement. This was in keeping with JP's own views, but another aspect of Gandhi's teachings—on the virtues of *brahmacharya* or abnegation of the sexual appetite—was another matter for a young man who had remained faithful to his wife despite the temptations and provocations of America and American life.

But Prabhavati had made up her mind long before he returned. Gandhi had dissuaded her from taking the vow in her husband's absence. So she had written to him and he had suggested that they put off a decision till he got back. In any case, he had pointed out, circumstances had imposed chastity on them due to his long stay abroad. She was still as determined when he returned, arguing persuasively that the question was not so much of adopting brahmacharya as a cult (she never took a formal vow) but of their mutual resolve to devote their lives to the service of the country. This would not be possible if they had children. He agreed, but many of his friends and colleagues were very critical of Gandhi for instilling such "unnatural" ideas into a young married woman. Prabhavati responded that the decision was her own and Gandhi had tried to dissuade her, but obviously her long stay at the ashram in the most formative years of her life influenced her thinking, and his commitment to brahmacharya was well known. She was a

The Young Congressman

determined young woman and continued to spend much of her time at the ashram while JP toured the country for one cause or another and shared a few rooms in Patna with his veteran socialist friend Ganga Sharan Sinha in between. She also remained a convinced Gandhian and was not influenced by JP's Marxist views.

Though Gandhi must have been pleased that Prabhavati had accepted his views, he did not want to impose them on JP as well and went to the length of suggesting that he should take another wife if he wanted to live a normal family life. JP turned down the suggestion saying that he and Prabhavati had decided to work out the relationship, but she upbraided Gandhi for thinking that her husband was too weak to live a life of celibacy. Having accepted the relationship, JP was determined to work it out. It must have imposed severe strains on him, from which he escaped by plunging even more deeply into political activity. All the same, it added to the complexity of his relationship with Gandhi.

JP was far from an uncritical admirer of Gandhi's politics and strategy. He did not attend his prayer meetings, though Prabhavati did. His sense of nationalism was too strong to accept the extreme position adopted by M. N. Roy who had criticized Lenin to his face for believing that because Gandhi was leading a mass movement he was a revolutionary. Roy had insisted that Gandhi was bound to be a reactionary socially because in his view he was a religious and cultural revivalist. This thesis was in fact accepted after Lenin's death. Roy changed his own views as he matured and before his death came to the JP-like conclusion that political parties prevented people from exercising their sovereignty and were an obstacle to democracy.

JP was still committed to the orthodox Marxist belief in violence, class conflict, and expansion of state power to impose socialism. None of these concepts was acceptable to Gandhi.

But JP had begun to have doubts about the Soviet model as reports of mass purges, deportation and liquidation of Kulaks began to flow in. Unlike the Soviet experience, he wanted the transition in his country to be gradual, without resort to coercion, but by using propaganda, example, subsidy and preferential taxation. But he still admired the Russians for what he believed they had achieved. And his disenchantment with Indian communists took the line that they had strayed from the correct Marxist approach but might return to it. He persisted with this belief—and the communists played upon it—for more than a decade, although it enabled them to do lasting injury to him and those who supported him. This was rooted in his conviction that the individual could rise above the system.

His independent approach also emerged in his advocacy of the village rather than the commune as the most suitable unit for cooperative and collective farming and his rejection of automation as unsuited to Indian conditions. His experiences in the United States had led him to oppose the concept of large impersonal individual cities. Instead he wanted industry to be diffused. In a few years, this would lead to his projection of the medium-sized agro-industrial village, combining the interdependence of rural life with the technical advantages of the city, as the ideal unit for social and economic development.

Despite their differences, there was thus enough in common between them to draw Gandhi and JP closer. They travelled together from Wardha to attend the Lahore session of the Congress in December 1929 at which Jawaharlal Nehru was elected president at the age of 40, in succession to his father Motilal. It was at this session that the Congress pledged to achieve total independence for the first time, the resolution being adopted at midnight on 31 December, after a delaying action by the conservatives. It was at Wardha that JP met Jawaharlal Nehru who was there to attend a pre-session working committee meeting.

The Young Congressman

Nehru introduced himself to JP, who had long admired him as the symbol of the young progressive wing of the Congress. Their views were very similar at this stage. Nehru took to the brilliant young Marxist, 13 years his junior, straightaway.

It was not too difficult to dissuade JP from proceeding any further with the idea of teaching at Banaras when Nehru offered him a paid job in the Labour Research Bureau of the All India Congress Committee office at Allahabad, where he stayed with the Nehrus. His relations with Jawaharlal became close enough for him to address him as "Bhai," a style he retained even when referring to Nehru more than forty years later in his abrasive correspondence with his daughter. Prabhavati became an even closer friend and confidante of Kamala Nehru who had nobody else in whom she could confide in the Westernized Nehru household.

The widespread feelings of disenchantment and doubt about Gandhi's non-violent tactics and goals disappeared when he launched a countrywide civil disobedience movement on 6 April 1930 after the dramatically symbolic build-up of the Dandi salt march. Gandhi, Nehru, and hundreds of Congress workers were arrested and some of them brutally beaten in jail. Hearing of this, JP's ailing mother pleaded with him to return home. He did, reluctantly, but set off again for Patna. His mother followed him; the strain proved too much and she died. His father too was semi-paralyzed and needed financial support in his illness.

Torn between his duty to his family and his desire to join the non-cooperation movement, and anguished by a feeling of guilt for his mother's death, JP wrote to Gandhi seeking his advice. The reply was prompt: in the circumstances his duty lay with his family. This was followed by a letter to Ghanshyam Das Birla, the industrialist, asking if he could find a job for JP. Birla responded by appointing him his private secretary.

The job did not go too well. JP was expected to research and write Birla's speeches. He did his job but not too enthusiastically.

The speeches had none of the elegantly simple and direct style of JP's political theses. Birla found him depressed. He was still in the grip of conflict between family and political ties. The Marxist in him resented working for a capitalist. The fact that Birla had come to his help in his time of need did not make things easier.

This unhappy phase ended with the Gandhi-Irwin or Delhi pact on 4 March 1931, which enabled the Congress Party to begin functioning openly and legally again. Nehru recalled JP and gave him the task of writing the history of the civil disobedience movement. But the truce with the government did not last long. Bhagat Singh, the young revolutionary who had been found guilty of killing a policeman and throwing a smoke bomb into the central legislative assembly, was executed within days of the pact being signed in spite of a countrywide campaign for commutation of the sentence. Even so, the Congress authorized Gandhi at its Karachi session to represent it at the second Round Table conference in London. Before he sailed in August, Lord Willingdon had replaced Irwin and a new wave of repression and arrests began. The conference dragged on for months, while the tension increased. Finally Gandhi sailed for home.

Jawaharlal Nehru left Allahabad for Bombay by train on 26 December 1931 to receive Gandhi and attend a CWC meeting. Since he knew he could be arrested because he had been served with a notice directing him not to leave Allahabad, he entrusted all his papers to JP who travelled in a separate compartment. As expected, the train was stopped at a wayside station and Nehru was arrested. JP went on to Bombay, where, dressed as a Parsi to avoid arrest, he delivered the papers to the acting Congress President, Sarojini Naidu. Soon after, on 4 January 1932, all Congress organizations were banned and the senior leaders arrested; in Allahabad, Prabhavati, too, was arrested along with Kamala Nehru on 3 February, and sentenced to two years imprisonment.

With the senior leaders in jail, more responsibility fell on JP, who became acting General Secretary of the party. Arrangements had been made for relatively junior Congress leaders to take over organizational work in the various provinces as their seniors were arrested, and for couriers to carry secret instructions and news of the movement to provincial units so that workers would not feel isolated. It now became his job to keep local units informed of the next phase of the civil disobedience movement and see that the reserve organization functioned. To do this, he travelled incognito round the country three times and attended a secret meeting of the unarrested and substitute members of the Congress Working Committee in Banaras.

At this time, the India League in Britain sponsored a delegation headed by Miss Ellen Wilkinson of the Labour Party to look into the charges of official brutality and suppression in dealing with the Congress movement. JP accompanied them on behalf of the party. He travelled openly even though warrants of arrest were pending against him in many provinces because it was believed that he would not be arrested when accompanying a British delegation. Nevertheless, he was arrested on 7 September 1932, when the group arrived in Madras and was sent to Bombay and from there to jail in Nasik, a small pilgrimage centre 120 miles from Bombay. With its quiet environment Nasik was a convenient place to detain political prisoners. The *Free Press Journal* of Bombay headlined the report of his arrest, "Congress Brain Arrested."

CHAPTER FIVE

CSP—BIRTH OF A PARTY

HIS FIRST jail term in Nasik was to prove as much of a landmark in JP's life as his stay at the University of Wisconsin where he became a convert to Marxism and a sympathizer of the Communist Party. He had been unhappy with the more brutal and authoritarian aspects of the Soviet experience for some time. This was increased by the shift in the Communist line on nationalist movements in colonial countries. Lenin's sympathetic attitude and united front tactics were reversed in 1928 by the Communist International under Stalin. The latest party line was to denounce Gandhi and the national movement as bourgeois and reactionary. Obediently, the Communist Party of India pulled out of all joint organizations, including trade unions, thus dividing the political as well as the labour movement. All this weakened JP's confidence in Moscow and the CPI, but he remained a Marxist.

As was to happen again in the future, the new line led the CPI to cooperate with the government against the national movement. Communist prisoners were freed while the jails were filled with Congressmen. Among those detained at Nasik with JP were some of the most articulate younger proponents of various shades of socialism outside the Communist Party—Asoka Mehta, Minoo Masani, Achyut Patwardhan, N. G. Goray, M. L. Dantwala. JP was just 30, but was treated as an elder. Asoka Mehta was only 21. They had little to do except discuss politics and get to know each other. Out of these fervent discussions emerged the concept of a Congress Socialist Party pledged to infuse the freedom movement with socialist ideals and to combine the forces of pure nationalism and economic revolt. Other young socialists, in other jails, were thinking on similar lines. Among them was Yusuf Meherally, a year younger than JP but better known in western India for his ability to inspire and organize students and young people. He came to public notice when, in the face of repeated lathi charges, he led a demonstration against the Simon Commission, which the Congress had decided to boycott, soon after it landed in Bombay. His convivial spirit helped to keep socialist intellectuals together in spite of personal angularities. His premature death in 1949 removed this common link.

After his release, JP hurried to organize his first relief mission in Bihar which had been devastated by the earthquake of 15 January 1934. Then he went on to organize a conference to set up the new party at Patna, where a lifelong colleague, Ganga Sharan Sinha, had already set up a provincial Socialist Party in 1932. The young socialists had become very concerned about recent trends in the Congress. The civil disobedience movement was petering out. The Swaraj Party—a constitutionalist group that was anxious to enter provincial legislatures in spite of their limited powers—was regaining strength under the eloquent leadership of Bhulabhai Desai, B. C. Roy and M. A. Ansari. This group had little concern for peasants and workers and preferred moving resolutions in legislative assemblies to participating in mass struggles. This was directly opposed to the views held by JP and his comrades who opposed any compromise with the British. So they called a conference in Patna on 17 May 1934, a day before the All India Congress Committee was scheduled to meet to call off the civil disobedience campaign formally and permit Congressmen who wanted to contest elections to do so.

Acharya Narendra Deva, an outstanding Marxist theoretician and a respected teacher of Kashi Vidyapith, 13 years older than JP and already a respected socialist elder, was an obvious choice for chairman. Although unhappy with the latest trend in the Congress, he stressed the need to work within it because he felt that it was the only organization with the popular backing required to achieve independence. But the key role was played by JP. His organizing ability and the clarity of his thinking had made him widely known among political workers. Even more, his evident sincerity and integrity combined to make him a national figure at the age of 32. This was evident in the resolution that was adopted. It said:

> In the opinion of this conference, the time has come for an all India organization of the Socialists in the Congress to be established. With this object in view, it is resolved that a drafting committee consisting of the following be appointed to prepare a draft programme and constitution of the Congress Socialist Party: Acharya Narendra Deva—President; Jayaprakash Narayan—Secretary; C. C. Banerjee and Faridul Huq—members.
>
> It is further resolved that Shri Jayaprakash Narayan be appointed the Organising Secretary of the All India Congress Socialist Conference to organise provincial Congress Socialist groups where they do not exist on the basis of the programme adopted by the drafting committee and arrange an all-India conference to form an all-India Congress Socialist Party immediately prior to the next session of the All India National Congress.

At the AICC meeting next day, Gandhi tried to keep everyone happy by supporting the Swaraj Party's effort while at the same time reiterating the view that he did not believe that the legislative assembly could be an instrument to achieve Swaraj. Having received his assent, the AICC went on to set up an election board to select candidates and supervise elections to the assemblies. The government responded by lifting the ban on Congress organizations. Later the Congress Working Committee went on to condemn "loose talk" of class war and confiscation of property as leading to violence. The socialists were the obvious target.

JP was quick to respond: "The resolution of the Congress Working Committee regarding the Congress Socialist movement shows how reactionary the present leadership of the Congress has become. The programme adopted by the Patna Socialist Conference speaks not of class war but of organising the masses on the basis of their economic interest and fighting for the removal of their immediate demands and leading them to independence and socialism. Nowhere in the Patna Conference had the phrase confiscation of property occurred."

Such phrases had not been used, but the resolution on the CSP's proposed objectives was pretty radical. The first item was vague enough to mean anything: "Power to be transferred to the producing masses," but others were more specific, for instance: "Development of the economic life of the country to be planned and controlled by the State," "Socialisation of principal industries with a view to progressive socialisation of all instruments of production, distribution and exchange," "Promotion of cooperation and collective farming with a view to the ultimate collectivisation of all agriculture," and "State monopoly of foreign trade." The resolution was moved by Minoo Masani, who in course of time would move to the other extreme in his views on economic development, would, in fact, become Swatantra Party leader.

These might have been treated as empty slogans of the kind that the Congress itself would adopt later, but the conference showed it meant business by passing a resolution expressing support for the textile strike then under way in Bombay. This antagonized the financiers of the Congress Party more than anything else.

While JP was organizing the CSP as a means to remedy the faults he found in the Congress, Gandhi was readying his own device to express unhappiness with trends within it. The reasons for his unhappiness were not entirely the same as JP's. What was more important, however, in shaping JP's future was the method he used to disentangle himself from the Congress while continuing to influence it. On 17 September Gandhi issued a statement confirming reports that he had decided to resign from the Congress Party. He did not join or form any other party because he felt he could contribute more by remaining outside the party structure—a decision that JP would take 20 years later.

At this stage, however, their views were very different. But the reason given by Gandhi for his resignation would sound familiar later—"The growing corruption in our ranks." Other reasons Gandhi gave for his resignation included the lack of enthusiasm for the charkha and khadi, symbols that JP had openly criticized.

Gandhi also referred to the decision to form the CSP. "I have welcomed the formation of the Socialist Group," he said. "Many of them are respected and self-sacrificing co-workers. With all this, I have fundamental differences with them on the programme published in their authorised pamphlets. But I would not, by reason of the moral pressure I may be able to exert, suppress the spread of ideas propounded in their literature." Another reason he gave was the reluctance of Congress leaders to commit themselves unequivocally to non-violence (not only JP but Jawaharlal Nehru also preferred the phrase "peaceful and legitimate means").

From the outset, the CSP stood for complete independence and separation from the British Empire in contrast to the many Congressmen who limited their demand to dominion status or less. But English officials were not too unhappy with the emergence of the new party. The sophisticated line they took—before the CSP gathered momentum—is evident from a message sent by an official of the Madras government to the Home Secretary in New Delhi in August 1934: "One

Jayaprakash Narayan, Organizing Secretary of the All India Congress Socialist Party, recently visited Madras city with a view to forming a provincial party for Tamil Nadu. The question of prosecuting him for an objectionable speech which he delivered on the 27th was raised, but the Madras Government decided not to do so because, among other reasons, his activities were likely to embarrass the Congress as much as, or more than, the Government. The Government also considered prosecution inadvisable in view of the smallness of the audience. ..."

The Congress Socialist Party was formally inaugurated at a convention in Bombay on 21 and 22 October 1934, on the eve of the annual Congress session. It was attended by 150 delegates, among whom were many who would leave a mark on the evolution of the independence movement as well as on indigenous socialist thinking—Ram Manohar Lohia, Achyut Patwardhan, Kamaladevi Chattopadhyaya, Minoo Masani, Purushottamdas Trikamdas. Sampurnanand, who would be a Congress chief minister of UP and a governor of Rajasthan, presided. The communists made their attitude clear by piling demonstrators into a truck and driving past the site of the convention at Worli, shouting slogans against the new party.

Fifty delegates had met at Banaras earlier in the month to work out their strategy and programme. To begin with, they condemned the AICC decision to contest elections to the legislative assembly as a drift towards "sterile constitutionalism." Then they defined their own attitude. They would concentrate on organizing peasant and labour unions to develop a mass movement and would oppose any move to discuss constitutional issues with the British Government. Their goal would be total independence. The preference for mass movements over electoral or legislative activity was a theme that would recur.

JP's stamp was evident on the organization as well as the

policies of the emerging CSP. The content of his political thinking had been refined by his recent experiences. The phase of uncritical communism was over: Stalin's policies and the CPI's behaviour had obliged him to distinguish communist strategy from Marxist principle. But he still held up achievements in the Soviet Union as a model. For he had begun to realize that little could be expected from the Congress. It was already evident that most of the lawyers, industrialists and landlords who supported the party were only thinking in terms of taking over the privileges enjoyed by their colonial masters, not of breaking out of the social injustice and economic immobilism that shackled Indian society.

During the civil disobedience movements he had seen poor peasants and workers lose everything while the rich paid their fines and saved their property. Many of the rich textile magnates who had readily financed the Congress boycott of foreign cloth lost their enthusiasm when they had exhausted their own stocks. Marxism still seemed to provide the only solution for the country's social ills. Gandhi's hold on popular opinion was a fact he recognized, but he did not accept his commitment to non-violence or decentralization of power.

On the other hand, he, too, did not confine himself to advocating only revolutionary remedies for misgovernment. Then, as later, the prisons of Bengal were full of revolutionaries and terrorists, and hundreds of others detained on the excuse that they were, or had consorted with, terrorists. So, in his presidential address to the Bengal CSP conference held in September 1935, we find him suggesting that "a non-political association should be formed, the business of which should be to defend the ordinary rights of citizenship—rights that are enjoyed by every member of any civilised society....It should be formed not of political workers but of leading jurists in the country; eminent publicists and journalists; women workers (for women are the worst sufferers); social workers like some of those of the

Servants of India Society, and so on. It should be an all-India body and should have intimate contacts with kindred foreign organisations. It should collect facts; publish literature; organise legal defence, raise funds for sufferers; do foreign propaganda; cause questions, resolutions etc. to be asked in the legislature and so on."

He would be making the same appeal when the jails of Bihar and West Bengal were full 40 years later. Had the analysis he made in his address of the reasons for tension between Hindus and Muslims in Bengal been accepted, much suffering could have been avoided: "The communal question in Bengal, as in other parts of the country, is largely an economic question and has resulted from the fact that the Muslims are nearly all tenants, and the landlords are nearly all Hindus. There has always been a serious conflict between the Bengal tenant and landlord; and peasant uprisings have been quite frequent here. But since the class division nearly coincides with the communal division, this conflict and these clashes have often been given a communal colour."

"Why Socialism," a thesis published in 1936 provided the most comprehensive review of his political and economic thinking at the time. It was a landmark in scope and clarity of writing. Among those it influenced was E. M. S. Namboodiripad who was later to become the first communist chief minister of an Indian state—Kerala. According to EMS, his education in socialism began with "Why Socialism."

At this stage, JP was still a firm Marxist and an admirer of Soviet achievements, though not uncritically. His views on parliamentary democracy, for instance, are stated in terms that bear the impress of black-and-white Marxism: "It was with the appearance of the ballot box and the party system of government that the fiction of democracy came into being. These two institutions were supposed to have conferred power on the whole people, equally on the lowest and the highest. But the economic order which weighs the scale too heavily on the side of the propertied interests, makes of this democracy a mockery. The rich have their great resources, their huge election funds, their great newspapers, their schools and colleges. And the poor? Well, they can have their dole or jolly well starve. The right to exercise the vote in these conditions means little to the workers."

As for the Soviet Union, although troubled by some of its excesses, it still seemed to represent a breakthrough in terms of corporate planning and social purpose replacing the individual will, and he held it up as a model in the most lyrical language: "What this may mean to man—to masses of men and women—may best be seen by turning to Russia, where a faith and a spirit seem to have been awakened for which neither the sky nor the sea, the wind nor river, remains unconquerable. To think that only a few years back this country was one of darkest despair, and most oriental lethargy!" He saw the Soviet Union as proof of the success of the thesis he advocated in the clearest language: "The essentials of economic planning are that production, distribution and saving (in the form of State investments) are properly adjusted and that all three march along a road carefully laid out in advance in accordance with the resources, equipment and needs of the people. The fundamental requirement is that there should be no private economic interests, separate from the social interest, between which a clash might develop."

Even then, however, he was not oblivious of the danger of over-centralized and imposed uniformity. But he defended the Soviet experiment in the belief that "Russia seems most anxious to avoid centralisation of economic control. The country has already been divided into autonomous geographical units of production with autonomous freedom and full creative initiative." He also noted that "a common prejudice regarding planned economy is that under it every individual would be dictated as to the articles he should wear and eat and the manner in which he should live." But his rejoinder was, "this as a matter of fact is true rather of capitalism than of planned life under Socialism."

His model for the takeover of private industry was admirably specific: "Let us see what exactly would happen by taking over one industry. Take cotton. A decree would be issued announcing that the eighty-odd mills of Bombay (let us take Bombay alone for an illustration) have become the property of the Indian people. A Cotton Industries Department would be set up to run the factories in conjunction with the representatives of the workers in the industry and in accordance with the National Economic Plan. The Department would decide, in accordance with that Plan, how much cotton should be bought and what manner and quantity of cotton goods should be manufactured in order to fulfil the needs of the community within its existing resources."

His views on agriculture, of which he had personal experience, showed much more individualism. He was as eager as any Marxist to put an end to the traditional exploitation of the cultivator by big landlords and moneylenders, but he showed more awareness of rural sentiment. Advocating redistribution of land, he explained: "Common ownership being our goal, it would appear rather strange that we should think of redistributing land to peasants. This necessity arises from the fact that common ownership and cultivation of land would be slow to develop and therefore we will have to begin with peasant proprietorship."

He also found indigenous rather than foreign inspiration for his thesis. His base unit was what he called "the old Indian village commune," and explained, "there were long periods of Indian history and long tracts of Indian territory in which a form of village existed—whatever its origin—in which common tenure of land and sometimes even common tillage were recogniszd and practised. In Madras such villages existed till the other day. The socialist aim follows in spirit the lines of the old system—except that the socialist village, instead of being a closed circle, a closed economic unit, would be an actively cooperating unit in a longer economic system."

And then, of course, he warned: "Let us be slow instead of hasty as the Russians. Let us use no coercion. Nor does the Party (CSP) advocate forcible socialisation of agriculture, as it does of industry. *Encouragement and promotion* (emphasis in the original) of cooperative and collective farming is the phrase used." But he did not mean to be over-critical of the experiment. "Let us make fewer mistakes than the Russians, if we are wise enough to avoid them. Remember, it is easy to be wise after the event. Let not the Russians' mistakes blind us to their great achievements, to the lessons they are teaching. . . ."

Politics was still totally identified with power politics. His approach was the same as that of his critics who could not later on comprehend his desire to change society without seizing power. "When the State is in your hands, you can legislate, you can use the whole magnificent apparatus of propaganda and education that modern science has made available; you can enforce your will. And if there is resistance, you can use the coercive arm of the State—the police and the army—to crush it. Behind every piece of legislation lies the State's power to persuade and, ultimately, to coerce. No party in the world today can build up Socialism unless it has the machinery of the State in its hands."

The programme he suggested to achieve economic freedom, to end exploitation, was also entirely Marxist and he would modify it in the coming years. The remedy he then proposed, in common with other Marxists, for the evils of private ownership was State ownership and control. He drew no distinction at that stage between "socialization" and "state control."

But a theme that would persist was his concept of the urbo-rural community which would share the advantages of village and city and the disadvantages of neither. His condemnation of modern cities seemed more a reaction to Chicago and New York than Bombay or Calcutta: "These monsters of human habitation—their crowding, their nerve-racking traffic, their insanitation, their slums—rightly make us revolt against them.... Further, the modern cities have grown on the exploitation of the people....The conditions of this exploitation bring about an unnatural hostility between city and village, in which the latter invariably gets the worse deal....Neither the socialist village nor the socialist city will bear any resemblance to its present prototype.

"Under socialism the cities will be planned and concentration avoided, because industry will be diffused. There will be geographical planning as well as statistical. On the other hand the villages will be transformed from clusters of houses—cut off from the world, tucked away within the recesses of the earth—to progressive communities, connected to the rest of the world with electricity, railways, telephones, radios, roads, buses. The village, too, will become an industrial unit of production like the city. It will be its self-government, its schools, its recreation centre, its museum."

CHAPTER SIX

THE COMMUNIST BETRAYAL

WITH THE formation of the CSP, JP's life was devoted to encouraging groups of like-minded radicals throughout the country to set up branches and, at the same time, organizing and strengthening urban workers' and peasants' associations. This went on for more than five years, years which were marked on the ideological and tactical planes by reactions and responses to Congress and Communist Party moves. But it did not take that long for him and his party to become too influential to be overlooked.

In the Congress, the attraction of ministerial office rapidly obliterated the previous commitment to mass struggle. The process was strengthened by the increased autonomy provided by the Government of India Act of 1935. The CSP continued to emphasize mass struggle and passed a resolution at its second conference at Meerut in January 1936 urging the Congress to wreck the new constitution.

In April that year, it seemed that the socialists would get a chance to influence the policies of the parent organization when Jawaharlal Nehru returned from Europe, after his wife Kamala's death, and was once more elected Congress president at the Lucknow session. Nehru was more impressed than ever by Soviet achievements and much of the communist ideology, and did not disguise his unhappiness with the increasingly conservative trend in the Congress. He promptly appointed three leading members of the CSP—Narendra Deva, JP, and Achyut Patwardhan—to his working committee. Ram Manohar Lohia was appointed to head the AICC's Foreign Affairs Department. Always correct, JP resigned the office of CSP general secretary. But even with their support Nehru was in a minority and after a few characteristic outbursts, including an offer to resign, he adjusted to the situation and by December was even advising CSP members "to speak of socialism in the language of India."

Nothing could now keep the Congress from seeking power, even under the limitations of the 1935 Act. The Faizpur session of the Congress, where Nehru was re-elected president in December 1936, paved the way for contesting elections to provincial assemblies early the following year. The Congress won an absolute majority in five provinces and was the biggest single party in four others. It did badly only in two. The process of verbal quibbling that would enable it to accept office in five provinces by July began immediately. The working committee authorized newly-elected members of the legislatures to take the oath of allegiance to the British sovereign. Even more hypocritical was the policy it laid down which tried to combine its previous revolutionary stand with accepting office: "The Congress has entered the legislature not to cooperate with the new Constitution or the Government but to combat the Act and the policy underlying it, as this Act and policy are intended to tighten the hold of British imperialism in India and to continue the exploitation of the Indian people. The Congress adheres to its general and basic policy of non-cooperation with the apparatus of British imperialism except in so far as circumstances may require a variation."

It was no surprise that JP found himself unable to continue as a member of the Congress Working Committee in these circumstances. He resigned within a few months and took over again as general secretary of the CSP, convinced even more than before that it needed to be strengthened further to be able to influence Congress policies.

In an article in the *Congress Socialist* in December 1936, JP gave vent to his frustration with the Congress leadership for avoiding social and economic problems and with aspects of Gandhi's approach in typically vigorous and clear language:

"Independence cannot be separated from its content. Therefore, to put socialism and independence in watertight compartments, to deny that any relation exists between them, is to weaken the fight for independence itself. No one says that our immediate fight is for socialism and yet socialism is the warp and woof of the immediate fight. It colours it, it gives it direction, it provides it with an edge of idealism. Men must know where they are going before they can take their steps firmly. Men fight and sacrifice their lives not for the first things they see before their noses but for ultimate ideals and objectives."

And in a flank attack on Gandhian tactics: "How shall we learn that imperialism cannot be overthrown by the manufacture of salt or picketing of liquor shops? From experience—our own and of others."

In his anxiety to counter what he viewed as the forces of reaction, JP was tempted to combine with the communists in the pursuit of "Socialist unity." This was made attractive by a shift in communist strategy in 1936 carried out under instructions from the Comintern, which, shaken by the Nazi victory in Germany, suddenly changed to the Popular Front line. Overnight the independence movement led by the Congress ceased to be an exclusively bourgeois preoccupation, it became an anti-imperialist national front and the CSP was no longer described as a "social fascist" organization. JP, always reluctant to doubt other's motives, was taken in and insisted on the acceptance of communists by the CSP. He still regarded himself as a staunch Marxist and was anxious to join hands with other Marxists who he felt had been led astray. He was joined by an even stauncher Marxist, Narendra Deva, but was strongly opposed by the group of younger socialists headed by Achyut Patwardhan, Minoo Masani, Ram Manohar Lohia and Asoka Mehta. The youger group submitted more out of their affection for JP than respect for his views, but later resigned from the national executive in protest. The communists, with S. A.

Dange among them, were not only admitted to the CSP but given key positions in it. Communists were also elected to the AICC with CSP support. They worked together in the trade union field. All this was most convenient to the Communist Party because it was unable to function openly after 1934 when it was banned.

The history of the CSP in the late thirties is a record of JP's reluctance to recognize the fact that his communist comrades were entering the party with the intention of infiltrating and taking over as many branches as possible while discrediting the original CSP leadership. Within a year of the communists being admitted, the CSP Executive Committee felt obliged in 1937 to warn provincial units against their "fractional" tactics. Soon after, the Communist Party denied CSP's claim to be a Marxist socialist party. Faced with this ideological attack, the executive stopped the admission of more communists into the CSP, but JP insisted that this "did not mean breaking off of friendly relations" and to "reiterate in no uncertain terms our continued desire for a united front between our two parties."

The Communist Party tried to make amends but, meeting at Calcutta in late 1937, the CSP executive decided that its explanation was inadequate. It made a third attempt soon after. And JP interpreted this as "recognising their mistake and accepting the Marxist Socialist character of the CSP." But even he had to concede that lack of harmony continued.

As late as 30 April 1939, the *Congress Socialist* published a joint May Day statement by JP and communist theoretician P.C. Joshi which read as if it had been drafted by the latter. It described the Soviet Union as "The Socialist Fatherland of the workers and toiling people of the whole world" and went on: "The working class of India and the whole people this day pledge their honour to defeat any imperialist-fascist war plans against the USSR." At home, threats to left unity were decried and "Socalist-Communist unity" specifically stated to be "the bedrock of left unity and the main lever of the United National Front."

When his old friend and colleague Ganga Sharan Sinha tried to keep the communists out of the CSP executive, JP even went to the extent of unilaterally and unconstitutionally increasing its membership by four to accommodate them. This tendency to take snap decisions without consulting his colleagues would create more problems later. Communist justification of the Soviet invasion of tiny Finland, and the party's reneging on an assurance to JP concerning the resolution that led to Subhas Bose resigning presidentship of the Congress at its Tripuri session in 1939, led to some disenchantment. It enabled the communists to gain popularity in Bengal at the cost of the CSP, which had earlier supported Bose against the conservative choice Pattabhi Sitaramayya. This increased as the communists put their "unity from below; opposition from above" slogan into effect, which meant winning over the CSP ranks while criticizing the leaders.

It was at the next Ramgarh Congress session in 1940 that the CSP executive decided to drop its four additional communist members. But the final break came only when Hitler attacked Russia in 1942 and what till then was an "imperialist war" for the communists became overnight a "people's war." The CSP never recovered fully from the communist embrace, especially in south India where virtually every branch had been infiltrated and taken over. It also lost control of several students' and workers' organizations.

JP remained a somewhat shaken Marxist, but he would never trust the Moscow-oriented communists again. Years later (in 1957) he described the bitter lesson learnt at so much cost "...that nightmare experience resulted in one great good. It taught us a great lesson in politics. We learnt, some of us with not a little regret, that there cannot be any unity with an 'official' communist party (that is, a party affiliated to the Comintern or approved by the Kremlin); that such a communist party is not a free agent but a tool; that the primary loyalty of the members of such a party is just to Russia and only then to anybody else; that when the communist parties talk of united front, it is always a ruse and at best a temporary policy dictated by the exigencies of the situation; that their unswerving goal is always monolithic communist rule; that the communists can never think of sharing power with anyone, except as a makeshift with convenient stooges."

His experience of the inner motivation of most Congress and Communist leaders further refined JP's political thinking and gave it the stamp of individuality. At the same time, the approach and outbreak of the Second World War, with the opportunist line taken by Britain and France in accepting the Nazi occupation of Czechoslovakia and by the Soviet Union in attacking Finland and signing a non-aggression pact with Hitler, made him more suspicious than ever of foreign intentions. Unlike Jawaharlal Nehru, he had no doubt about continuing to struggle against Britain's grip on India after it was engaged in fighting Nazi Germany. For him the European war was between rival schools of imperialism. This attitude persisted even after Russia was attacked. His sympathies were with the Soviet Union, but he saw no reason to relax the struggle against foreign rule over India.

At Tripuri, he had moved the National Demand resolution which specified, among other things, that nothing less than independence and a constitution drawn up by a constituent assembly elected on the basis of full adult franchise would be acceptable. The resolution was adopted, but the Congress leadership would go back on it in working out the arrangement for the transfer of power with the British Government. JP would remain consistent—to the extent of asking his socialist colleagues to boycott the constituent assembly set up under the agreement because it was elected on a limited franchise.

In spite of his criticism of Gandhi, he could not help being influenced by him more and more. The struggle between their views waxed and waned and did not really end until after Gandhi was dead and JP finally recognized the fatal flaw in Marxism—its leaving no room for ethical and moral considerations, the only motivation that can impel human beings to seek something beyond their individual well-being. But it was not only JP who modified his views; so did Gandhi, when persisting with them could lead to a major political reverse—as in sanctioning the Quit India movement when it was evident that it would not be totally non-violent and treating use of violence in a one-sided confrontation as non-violence: "If a man fights with his sword against a horde of dacoits armed to the teeth, I would say he is fighting non-violently."

At this stage, however, the gap was still wide. JP was critical of the pledge concerning khadi spinning and other aspects of the constructive programme that were asked of Congressmen on 26 January 1940. Gandhi replied sharply in *Harijan:* "If the majority of Congressmen entertain the view that Shri Jayaprakash propounds on behalf of the Socialist Party, I can never hope to lead such an army to success. He has no faith in the programme or the present leadership. . . .If I were in Shri Jayaprakash's place and if I felt able to tender discipline, I would advise my party to remain indoors and silent."

JP remained a Marxist, but the realization of his own previous errors of judgment and increased awareness of developments in the Soviet Union under Stalin gave his interpretation an even more humane aspect than before. He stressed, for instance, that Marx had taught that in certain circumstances it was not necessary to use violence to attain socialism. The impress of all these events at home and abroad was evident in a draft resolution sent by him to Gandhi to be put before the Ramgarh session of the Congress held in March 1940, six months after India had been dragged into the war by order of the Viceroy,

The Communist Betrayal

without even consulting the Congress, thus weakening those believing in constitutionalism and reviving the spirits of those who, like JP, placed more faith in mass struggle. All Congress governments in the provinces resigned within ten weeks of the outbreak of war.

JP's draft was not discussed at Ramgarh because the working committee decided to have only one political resolution. But Gandhi published it in *Harijan*, as requested by JP, with his comments. He gave general endorsement to all its propositions except one—that the titles and privileges of the rulers of the princely states would be abolished in free India. This, he felt, would be wrong because the rulers were independent in law and the process of democratization should be left to them. The draft itself was a remarkable document. It showed up clearly how far JP had moved from the strident sloganizing of the May Day statement of a year ago and the influences it represented. It also revealed the impress already made by Gandhi on the original Marxist cast of his political thinking. Concise and pointed in comparison with traditional Congress resolutions, it read:

The Congress and the country are on the eve of a great national upheaval. The final battle for freedom is soon to be fought. This will happen when the whole world is being shaken by mighty forces of change. Out of the catastrophe of the European war, thoughtful minds everywhere are anxious to create a new world—a world based on the cooperative goodwill of nations and men. At such a time the Congress considers it necessary to state definitely the ideals of freedom for which it stands and for which it is soon to invite the Indian people to undergo the uttermost sufferings.

The free Indian Nation shall work for peace between nations and total rejection of armaments, and for the method of peaceful settlement of national dispute, through some international authority freely established. It will endeavour particularly to live on the friendliest terms with its neighbours, whether they be great powers or small nations, and shall covet no foreign territory.

The law of the land will be based on the will of the people freely expressed by them. The ultimate basis of maintenance of the order shall be the sanction and concurrence of the people.

The free Indian State shall guarantee full individual and civil liberty and cultural and religious freedom provided that there shall be no freedom to overthrow by violence, the constitution framed by the Indian people through a Constituent Assembly.

The State shall not discriminate in any manner between citizens of the nation. Every citizen shall be guaranteed equal rights. All distinctions of birth and privilege shall be abolished. There shall be no titles emanating either from inherited social status or the State.

The political and economic organization of the State shall be based on principles of social justice and economic freedom. While the organization shall conduce to the satisfaction of the national requirements of every member of society, material satisfaction shall not be its sole objective. It shall aim at healthy living and the moral and intellectual development of the individual. To this end and to secure social justice, the State shall endeavour to promote small-scale production carried on by individual or cooperative effort for the equal benefit of all concerned. All large-scale production shall be eventually brought under collective ownership and control and in this behalf the State shall begin by nationalising heavy transport, shipping, mining and the heavy industries. The textile industry shall be progressively decentralised.

The life of the villages shall be reorganised and the villages shall be made self-governing units, self-sufficient in as large a measure as possible. The land laws of the country shall be drastically reformed, on the principle that land shall belong to the actual cultivator alone, and that no cultivator shall have more land than is necessary to support his family on a fair standard of living. This will end the various systems of landlordism on the one hand and farm bondage on the other.

The State shall protect the interests of all the classes, but when any of these impinges upon the interests of those who have been poor and downtrodden, it shall defend the latter and thus restore the balance of social justice.

In all State-owned and State-managed enterprises, the workers shall be represented in the management through their elected representatives and shall have an equal share in it with the representatives of the Government.

In the Indian states, there shall be complete democratic government established and in accordance with the principles of abolition of social distinctions and equality between citizens, there shall not be any titular head of the states in the persons of Rajahs and Nawabs.

This is the order which Congress envisages and which it shall work to establish. The Congress firmly believes that this order shall bring happiness, prosperity and freedom to the people of all races and religions in India who together shall build on these foundations a great and glorious Nation.

Not only was his resolution not discussed at the Ramgarh session; he was unable to attend it himself. He had not confined his opposition to India being dragged into the war to public statements: he opposed it actively. Two weeks before the session on 19 and 20 March, he was arrested for making a "seditious" speech at a strike meeting of workers at Jamshedpur, the heart of the country's steel industry. His behaviour at the trial closely followed the pattern set by Gandhi, from pleading guilty to thanking the English judge for his courtesy and consideration. His defence was also noteworthy for its clear stand on the war. In part it said :

I have been charged with trying to impede the production of munitions and other supplies essential to the efficient prosecution of the war, and with trying to influence the conduct and attitude of the public in a manner prejudicial to the defence of British India and the efficient prosecution of the war. I plead guilty to these charges.

These charges, however, do not constitute a guilt for me but a duty which I discharge, regardless of the consequences. That they also constitute an offence under certain laws of a fereign Government, established by force in this country, does not concern me .... My country is not party to this war in any manner, for it regards both German Nazism and British Imperialism as evils and enemies. Great Britain is fighting not to destroy Nazism, which it has nurtured, but to curb a rival, whose might can no longer be allowed to grow unchallenged ....As far as India is concerned, Great Britain is fighting to perpetuate the Indian Empire.

Plainly, India can have no truck with such a war. No Indian can permit the resources of his country to be utilised to buttress up imperialism and to be converted through the processes of the war into the chains of his country's slavery. The Congress, the only representative voice of nationalist India, has already pointed out this sacred duty to the people of this country. I, as an humble servant of the Congress, have only tried to fulfil this duty.

The British Government, on the other hand, in utter disregard for Indian opinion, has declared India a belligerent power and is utilising Indian men, money and materials for a war to which we have pledged our uncompromising opposition. This is in the nature of an aggression against India, no less serious in the circumstances than German aggression against Poland. India cannot but resist this aggression. It, therefore, becomes the patriotic duty of every Indian to oppose the attempt of the British Government to use the country's resources for its imperialist ends. Thus the charge framed against me of trying to impede the efficient prosecution of the war is only the fulfilment of a patriotic duty. That the British Government should consider what is a duty for patriotic India to be an offence, only proves further its imperialist character.

The government probably calculated that JP's arrest would enable the constitutionalist wing of the Congress to reassert its leadership. But Gandhi promptly and publicly interpreted it as provocation. In retrospect, his comment in *Harijan* can be seen as a warning to the Viceroy of the massive civil disobedience movement which took the shape of the Quit India campaign two years later. He said:

The arrest of Shri Jayaprakash is unfortunate. He is no ordinary worker. He is an authority on Socialism. It may be said that what he does not know of western Socialism nobody else in India does. He has forsaken all for the sake of the deliverance of his country. His industry is tireless. His capacity for suffering is not to be excelled . . . .

I have said before now that it is open to the Government to precipitate a crisis if they wish. They have every right to do so. But I have hugged the hope that the fight will be allowed to develop along its natural course so long as it is strictly non-violent. Let there be no camouflage. If Shri Jayaprakash is guilty of violence, violence should be proved. What the arrest has done is to make the people believe that the British Government want to force the issue. History will then have to repeat itself. During the first civil disobedience, the

Government had forced the issue by arresting the Ali brothers. Is this arrest a prearranged plan or is it a blunder committed by some over-zealous officer? If the latter, it should be set right.

It was not, and JP found himself back in jail.

CHAPTER SEVEN

QUIT INDIA

In contrast to his earlier incarceration in Nasik, the nine months JP spent in Hazaribagh jail in 1940 were marked by frustration combined with a sense of betrayal. Since mass arrests had not yet begun, he did not have the company of like-minded prisoners. And he was all too aware of the rapid march of events outside the thick walls of the jail. This mood led up to the role he would play in the 1942 movement.

It was a time when the Congress Party was riven by differences on the strategy to adopt towards the war. It also saw the development of the separatist move by M.A. Jinnah and the Muslim League, who seized the opportunity provided by the resignation of Congress ministries in the provinces to move closer to the Viceroy.

JP's solution for these problems was mass revolutionary struggle, which would sweep all those eager to maintain the *status quo*—the League and the conservatives in the Congress—away with the British. He regarded any move to reach an interim agreement with the British as betrayal because it would strengthen the conservatives in the country. Gandhi took a similar stand but for different reasons. An agreement with Britain would mean cooperating in the war and thus conflict with his belief in non-violence.

Nehru's links with the West and his anti-fascist background made him anxious to participate in the war against Hitler, provided it could be done with a measure of self-respect with national leaders somehow associated with the government. Abul Kalam Azad, who was Congress president, was less emotional. To him an offer to cooperate in the war was a bargaining counter to make Britain concede a scheduled programme for independence. C. Rajagopalachari (Rajaji) represented yet another approach. As a conservative, he wanted a slow, phased transfer of power with minimal repercussions on Indian society.

After the fall of France, when Nehru's sympathy for the Western democracies persuaded him to reduce the role he sought for the Congress in an interim government, Rajaji was able to persuade the AICC to adopt a resolution in July offering to cooperate in the war in return for a national government in New Delhi which would have no statutory powers and no say in the conduct of the war (no constitutional change in the Viceroy's status was envisaged until after the war). The resolution went through in spite of Gandhi's opposition—the first time this had occurred.

JP was scandalized. "Rajaji has stabbed us in the back," he wrote to Nehru from jail, pleading with him to resign from the working committee in protest. But Nehru had gone along with the resolution. JP spent the rest of his term in jail planning to go underground when he was released to organize a mass struggle for freedom before the conservatives reached a deal with the British.

But the British Government, now led by Winston Churchill, failed to respond to the Congress initiative. So a year after the war began, Gandhi tried a new tactic—individual civil disobedience. This would register India's resentment at being dragged into the war, without putting a strain on the administration. Contrary to the impression that Nehru would be given the honour of being the first satyagrahi, Gandhi chose a virtually unknown disciple who was destined to become a major influence on JP—Vinoba Bhave. Nehru was to be second, but was arrested on 31 October, before he could court arrest.

JP completed his sentence towards the end of the year. But at a time that the government felt it necessary to sentence Nehru to four years' imprisonment, he could not expect to stay out long. The police kept a close watch on him. Soon after he landed in Bombay to make plans for an underground campaign against the government, he was rearrested. The time there was no trial. He was detained indefinitely under the Defence of India Rules.

After a short spell in Bombay's Arthur Road prison, JP was sent to a temporary jail in Deoli, 80 miles from Ajmer, in the heart of Rajputana. Deoli was in a British-ruled enclave surrounded by princely states, which made it remote from political developments in British India. Originally set up to accommodate prisoners of war, it had few facilities, but was well guarded and run on military lines—arrangements well-suited for maximum security prisoners. There he had company, for the government had decided to detain all leftist and revolutionary prisoners in this isolated spot. Among them were communists and 38 Congress socialists.

This remote jail however was the scene of two events that would make JP more widely known, specially among the young, than anything he had done so far. They showed he could act as well as think. One occurred because JP was anxious to keep in touch with his comrades in preparing for a major confrontation with the government. He found a sympathetic junior jail official who agreed to smuggle messages out but then grew scared of being found out. One secret message was sent with a letter to his wife asking her to insert an apparently innocent sentence in her next letter to indicate that it had been received. When he received a letter from her after some time without the code sentence, he questioned the official, who confessed that he had not dared to smuggle the message out.

Impatiently, he sent word asking Prabhavati to seek an interview with him. She did, and under cover of handing her a sheet of paper with the outline of his foot on it—to get a new pair of slippers, he explained to the jail staff—he tried to hand her the packet as well. But a CID officer noticed, called the guard, and managed to grab the packet after a struggle. The government publicized the letter to portray him as a terrorist, adding that JP had described individual satyagraha as a farce. It hoped no doubt to turn Gandhi against him. But again it miscalculated. Gandhi put out a statement that defended JP without compromising his own stand on non-violence. And the publicity that the controversy created kept JP's name in the headlines.

The communique issued by the government on the incident said: "Plans to consolidate the position of the Congress Socialist Party by winning over important members of the terrorist organizations known as the Revolutionary Socialist Party and the Hindustan Republican Socialist Association and isolating the Communist Party were seized from Mr Jayaprakash Narayan, security prisoner, Deoli Camp, when he attempted to pass them to his wife, Prabhavati Devi, at an interview."

In the English translation that was published of JP's letter in Hindi to his wife, he gave her instructions on how to conceal messages in the binding of books sent to him in jail. ("Mark a plus sign on page 100 in pencil. I will open the binding of the book marked with this sign.") It suggested that a colleague, Basawan Singh, be told to go underground and recruit men for a secret wing of the CSP. They were asked to procure money by the "old method"—which was political dacoity, according to the government.

Five days later Gandhi issued a statement from Wardha. It said: "The publication of the statement attributed to Shri Jayaprakash Narayan, which he is stated to have attempted to smuggle from his place of detention, does not so far as I can see, lead us anywhere. If the motive was to discredit the organisation of which Shri Jayaprakash Narayan is a distinguished member, it must fail.

"Assuming the correctness of the charge against Jayaprakash Narayan, the method advocated by him is against the policy of truth and non-violence adopted by the Congress, and he deserves the severest condemnation. But it ill becomes the Government to condemn or discredit it. Frankly, all nationalist forces, no matter by what they are described, are at war with the government. And, according to the accepted canons of war, the method adopted by Jayaprakash Narayan is perfectly legitimate. He has had his training in America for seven years, and is a student of the methods adopted by Western nations in their fight for freedom. To practise deception, to resort to secret methods and even to plot murder, are all honourable and turn the perpetrators into national heroes. Are not Clive and Warren Hastings British heroes? If Jayaprakash Narayan was in the British Diplomatic Service and by secret diplomacy achieved something of importance, he would be covered with distinction.

"The sensation with which the event has been disclosed to the Indian world is ill-conceived. The annotations in the communique are probably wholly unwarranted. When it is borne in mind that Jayaprakash Narayan is an untried detenu, the annotations look very like hitting below the belt. The Government should have shown Jayaprakash the document or documents seized, and published his answer if he had one to give. . . .

"One word to Congressmen. While Jayaprakash Narayan remains the patriot we have known him, they must realise that this method is harmful in the extreme while a non-violent struggle is going on. I have said, repeatedly, that secrecy has no place in a non-violent organization. No underhand or underground movement can ever become a mass movement or stir millions to mass action. Indeed, I would appeal to Jayaprakash Narayan to reconsider his philosophy and if his reason can approve, to repudiate the method as a lapse from sound reason and the loyalty he owes to the Congress. What he has stigmatised as a farce of satyagraha is not a farce. It is the fine fruit of mature experience of thirty-three years experimenting in truth and non-violence; and if God wills it, I hope to demonstrate that from this farce, will rise a reality which will compel admission even by Jayaprakash Narayan and those who think with him. Jayaprakash did not indeed go to prison as a satyagrahi, but he has not ceased to be a member of the Congress, and so it is not proper for him and others who think with him to retard the movement by their action, which is admittedly disloyal to the Congress."

The statement also referred to the bad conditions in Deoli jail and suggested that it be disbanded. Complaints about the jail had been mounting and led to the second event that was widely publicized and helped to make JP known even more widely. This was a hunger-strike for an objective that Gandhi had mentioned —the closure of the Deoli jail. It lasted 31 days. Sympathy meetings were held throughout the country and the issue was discussed in the Central assembly. Finally the government climbed down and sent the detenus to jail in their home provinces. JP was now as famous as the most senior Congress leaders. His involvement in underground activities made him a bigger hero than any of them in youthful eyes.

The last provided another occasion for disillusionment with the communists. They had agreed to participate in the fast but pulled out after a few days. This was in keeping with the shift in their approach to the war after Hitler attacked Russia. Not long after, all communist detenues were released and the ban on the party was lifted.

JP was also concerned about the invasion of the Soviet Union which he still regarded as a stronghold of socialism despite its failings. But to him securing India's independence was not less important than helping Russia. While still in Deoli, he wrote: "Till the invasion of Russia, we had looked upon the war as an imperialist war. The recent action of Germany against Russia has in no way modified this position....If Russia and Britain are facing a common enemy it does not mean their interests coincide ... The danger which Russia faces however is a question which as socialists it is our duty to seriously consider. With all its faults, Soviet Russia is a giant fortress of world socialism and the proletariat. We cannot sit quiet while this fortress is under assault.... But it would be a mistake to relax our attack on imperialism."

The dilemma worried him for some time, but he decided that priority must be given to launching an extensive revolutionary movement to overthrow British rule quickly. Only when it was independent could India be an effective ally of the Soviet Union.

There was no such single-mindedness in the Congress leadership. Russia's involvement in the war imposed further strains on it, with the leftists becoming reluctant to embarrass the war effort. Gandhi's token satyagraha movement petered out well before the end of 1941. Nehru and most of the moderate Congress leaders were released from jail early in December. Then came Pearl Harbour, which made the war global, with far-reaching repercussions on British policy and Congress attitudes. After their release, the Congress leaders made another conditional offer of cooperation with the government in the war. This was in January 1942 by which time Nehru had made it clear that he did not share Gandhi's commitment to non-violence in defending the country. In fact, he described it as "preposterous."

Japan's rapid advance to Singapore and beyond made it seem possible that the British might be driven out of India. This sharpened the conflict within and outside the Congress. The followers of Subhas Bose, who had escaped from India a year previously and begun broadcasting from Berlin and later Tokyo, were anxious to use the opportunity to expel the British. But Nehru was most unhappy with the idea of cooperating with the Japanese.

The war came even nearer when the Japanese troops occupied Rangoon on 8 March. President Roosevelt had enhanced his efforts to persuade Winston Churchill to reach an agreement with Indian leaders after the United States entered the war. Reluctantly, the British Government despatched Sir Stafford Cripps to negotiate a settlement three days after Rangoon fell. As a left-wing Labour Party leader, who was a friend of Nehru, it was thought he would have the best chances of success. But the talks failed for a number of reasons; important among them was Gandhi's opposition, based on the same principle that JP had adopted—India's freedom must come first. This was the theme of a resolution adopted by the Congress Working Committee in July. The committee called a session of the All India Congress Committee, in which delegates from all provincial units would be present in

Bombay on 7 August.

Even Gandhi's monumental patience was coming to an end. "I waited and waited until the country should develop the non-violent strength necessary to throw off the foreign yoke," he said in a statement. "But my attitude has now undergone a change. I feel that I cannot afford to wait. If I continue to wait, I might have to wait till doomsday. For the preparation that I have worked and prayed for may never come, and in the meantime I may be enveloped and overwhelmed by the flames that threaten all of us. That is why I have decided that even at certain risks which are obviously involved, I must ask the people to resist the slavery." And to make his stand clear, he addressed these words to the Japanese: "We are in the unique position of having to face an imperialism that we detest no less then yours and Nazism."

Soon after, he even modified his views on non-violence: "Supposing a mouse fighting a cat tried to resist the cat with its sharp teeth, would you call that mouse violent? In the same way, for the Poles to stand bravely against the German hordes vastly superior in number, military equipment and strength, was almost non-violent."

Without consulting each other, for JP was in jail all this time, his and Gandhi's views had come close.

JP was back in Hazaribagh jail, after the closure of Deoli, when the AICC passed the Quit India resolution in Bombay on 8 August. It sanctioned "a mass struggle on non-violent lines on the widest possible scale." Gandhi, who had coined the slogan "Quit India" also described the movement as "unarmed revolt" and "open rebellion." Early next morning, he and all the Congress leaders assembled in Bombay, including party president Azad, Gandhi and Nehru, were rounded up and despatched to jail. The reaction was immediate—an explosion of popular anger against the government, mostly unplanned but to some extent aimed at sabotaging the movement of men and supplies in connection with the war. It was countered by maximum repression, including strafing from the air.

The official papers released by the British Government concerning the period reveal how much more serious the outburst was than admitted at the time. Bihar and eastern UP was the storm-centre. As early as 11 August, the Governor of Bihar reported to the Viceroy, that the people of Patna "through the night engaged in widespread sabotage and road obstruction, the thoroughness of which had to be seen to be believed.... With rail, telegraph and telephone communication out of order we lost immediate touch with other districts." The commissioner of Tirhut division had ordered the abandonment of less important police stations. The Tata Steel Works at Jamshedpur (where JP had been arrested more than two years earlier) was shut down because of a strike.

Four weeks later, the Commander-in-Chief gave a preliminary estimate of the impact of the Quit India movement. Training had been disrupted, he said, because the equivalent of 57 battalions had been posted on internal security duties and petrol supply dislocated. The movement programme for the eastern area had been retarded at least three weeks due to railway damage. Half the aerodrome construction programme had been disrupted as a result of shortages and labour difficulties. Ten per cent of Tata's annual steel production had been lost already due to the strike. The general effect of dislocation and unrest on the country's economy were having repercussions on military supplies and transportation.

While the Viceroy, Lord Linlithgow, whom Nehru described as "heavy of body and slow of mind," usually sent messages to London playing down the movement, a personal cable sent to Secretary of State Leopold Amery in September to ward off a proposed visit by US Vice-President Wendell Willkie revealed the real state of affairs. It began: "I am engaged here in meeting the most serious rebellion since that of 1857, the gravity and extent of which we have so far concealed from the world for reasons of military security." And it ended: "I feel bound to beg you to ginger up Edward Halifax (British Ambassador in Washington and as Lord Irwin, a former Viceroy) to arrest at least for a time, the flow of well-meaning sentimentalists from the USA to India so that we may mind here, what is still, I suppose, our own business."

II

To be confined in Hazaribagh—one of the few areas of Bihar not much affected by the movement because it was in a thickly forested tribal area—in a jail with thick 17-foot high walls, was acutely frustrating at such a time. The kind of revolt that he had worked for and hoped for had now been sanctioned by Gandhi himself. JP was closely watched in view of his activities in Deoli, but the desire to escape and take part in the revolt was overwhelming even though he had been far from well and was suffering from sciatica. Three months after the revolt began, he worked out a plan with five other prisoners, that was as carefully rehearsed as an escape from a POW camp.

The night chosen was Diwali, 9 November 1942, one of the darkest in the year. While the other prisoners sang, danced and lit the traditional oil lamps, the escape group gathered in a dark corner, waited till the sentry passed on his rounds and made a human ladder against the wall, one standing on the other's shoulders. JP was third in the chain. The last got his legs across the wall, threw down a rope made of knotted dhotis and helped the others over. They were over the wall in six minutes; the sentry completed his round in eight. But in the hurry, a package containing their shoes, extra clothing and money was left behind. Crippled by sciatica, JP had to be carried part of the way. After a few miles, a bullock-cart owner was persuaded to carry him and two others weakened by long spells of imprisonment.

A couple of days later the party split, three heading north and three west towards UP. JP was in the second group with Ramanandan Misra and Shaligram Singh, who was secretary of the Hazaribagh district Congress committee and knew the area well enough to guide them by a roundabout route to his father-in-law's village where they rested three days. They walked through Gaya and Shahabad districts, where it was JP's fluency in the Bhojpuri dialect that enabled them to pass off as local villagers, and on to a wayside station near Dehri-on-Sone where they boarded a crowded third class compartment of a train to Moghalsarai. It was only after they had crossed the Ganga by boat and got to Banaras that JP contacted some of the local Congress leaders. They decided to call a meeting of Congress leaders who had escaped arrest at Delhi. JP proceeded there by train, travelling first class in the guise of an ailing zamindar of Oudh. It was at the Delhi meeting that JP pushed through a plan to raise and train a guerrilla force to sabotage the war effort as a way to keep the Quit India movement alive.

The revolt had passed its peak by the time JP escaped and would be crushed, except in remote pockets, by the end of the year. But his exploits became an instant legend, to which the government contributed by offering first five and then ten thousand rupees for information leading to his capture. This did not prevent him from travelling in disguise by train around the country, appearing in major cities—including Bombay, Madras and Calcutta after Delhi—meeting old friends, addressing groups, making people feel that the revolt was still alive, before going underground again. Printed and cyclostyled pamphlets and newsletters were distributed, including two long and eloquent letters addressed "To all Fighters of Freedom," unmistakably written by him. A third letter to American soldiers in India appeared in several US military installations. It appealed to them "as soldiers of freedom to support us in our struggle for freedom" by "refusing to take any part in Britain's fascist war against us," and by telling their countrymen and government the real truth about India and making British soldiers aware of the facts.

Though written in rousing, emotional language, he did not conceal the truth in the letters to his countrymen. The first—written in early 1943—admitted that the rising had been suppressed and analyzed the reasons as lack of organization and failure to plan follow-up action. "After they had completely destroyed the British Raj in their areas, the people considered their task fulfilled, and went back to their homes not knowing what more to do.... They should have set up in their areas their own units of revolutionary government and created their own police and militia."

He was equally outspoken on the sensitive issue of violence versus non-violence. "I should have no hesitation in admitting," he wrote, "that non-violence of the brave, if practised on a sufficiently large scale, would make violence unnecessary; but where such non-violence is absent, I should not allow cowardice clothed in Shastric subtleties to block the development of this revolution and lead to its failure."

In the second letter, dated 1 September 1943, JP admitted that the second wave of the uprising that he had hoped for earlier had not materialized. But he still envisaged a protracted struggle. The primary objective was "creation of deadlock and paralysing and dislocation of British rule." But there was "no room for murder in it (the struggle), nor any form of violence to the person." Such a programme of struggle, he felt, was the only answer to the constitutional and communal problems that were blocking the way to independence. He justified the attempt by Subhas Bose to set up a national army with Japanese help but insisted that "our freedom largely depends on our own strength and resources....We must be ready in the event of an Axis-Allied clash in India to seize power ourselves. Only if we are ready to make this attempt can outside help such as Subhas' National Army be of value to us and Tojo be prevented from annexing India."

In the same letter, he hinted that "some progress has already been made in developing a guerrilla movement." This was the most romantic and least effective of his exploits. The training centre was on an island in the Kosi river near Bihar's border with Nepal. Here and in the wild terai area on both sides of the border was organized the Azad Dasta, with training in mining and blowing up roads and bridges, disrupting railway signal cabins and telephonic communication and in armed defence against attack. JP was seen with a revolver in his belt but was never known to have fired it. Prominent among those who joined him was Ram Manohar Lohia, whom he had contacted in Delhi.

But by this time, little was left of the revolt. The tiny guerrilla force had to slip back and forth across the Nepal border to escape capture. Even this became difficult when the Government of India managed to persuade the Nepal Government to take action against the force. Eventually JP and Lohia were surprised by a Nepalese police party and taken to Hanuman Nagar police station to be handed over to the Indian police. But a bigger Azad Dasta force of 35 men heard of the capture and besieged the police station. While shots were exchanged JP and Lohia escaped, with Lohia leaving his spectacles behind and having to be guided through the forest.

Several Nepalese constables were injured in the encounter and one died subsequently. JP felt very sad when he heard about this. The feeling of guilt was still with him nearly four years later when on 9 June 1947 he wrote to the Maharaja of Nepal explaining the circumstances in which the encounter took place and seeking permission to contribute two thousand rupees to the family of the guard who died. "... as our country was fighting for freedom and as we had been arrested in the course of that struggle at the insistence of the then government of India, we had to secure our freedom at any cost," he explained. "I take this opportunity to offer Your Highness personally and to your government my sincere regrets for that incident."

But that did not prevent him from urging the Maharaja to release political prisoners detained in the satyagraha recently condu-ct ed in Nepal and come to terms with the Nepali Congress which was agitating for representative government. He was concerned about the fate of the Koirala brothers, especially Bisheshwar Prasad, who was a close friend. Six weeks later, the Maharaja responded with a polite note informing JP that he need not worry because a pension had been awarded to the family of the guard who was killed and assuring him that the Koiralas would get a fair and just trial. (Thirty years later, JP was to make an almost identical appeal, again on behalf of B.P. Koirala, who had been detained as soon as he re-entered Nepal after eight years' self-exile. This time, the Nepalese Prime Minister responded with a hard-hitting attack on what he called a "hate Nepal campaign in responsible circles in India." He blamed, among others, "prominent leaders of the erstwhile Socialist Party," although JP had made it clear that his intention was not to interfere in the internal affairs of any country.)

As JP continued to go round the country trying to revive the Quit India movement, he came into touch with more and more people until the inevitable happened. Someone informed the police that he was travelling by train from Delhi to Rawalpindi by the Frontier Mail to contact Pathan insurgents in the North-West Frontier Province. The train was leaving Amritsar for Lahore on the morning of 19 September 1943, when one English and two Indian police officers entered his compartment and seized him at revolver point. The train was halted at Mughalpura, a small station just outside Lahore, which had been surrounded by police. A police party rushed JP to a cell in the old Mughal fort in Lahore where political prisoners were imprisoned and interrogated, and from where escape was impossible. He had been out of jail for just over ten months and would not be free again till April 1946, long after other national leaders were released.

Thus JP was in jail at a critical period of the negotiations leading to the partition of the country and the transfer of power.

The prolonged detention was worse than anything he had been through before. A month after his capture, when all available information about him had been collected from different provinces, interrogation began in the presence of CID officers from Bengal, Bihar and Punjab. He told them he would not answer any question concerning his underground activities; that he was working for his country's independence and would continue to do so. They made it clear that he would not be released until they got the information they wanted. He was not beaten (as were many other prisoners in the fort), but the hours of interrogation grew steadily longer until he was allowed no sleep for several days at a time. This continued until mid-December when the interrogation abruptly stopped and was not resumed.

Although he was not tortured this way again, the rest of his imprisonment in Lahore fort was a period of mental agony. He was confined alone in a small cell and let out, in handcuffs, for an hour of exercise morning and evening. His only source of information about events outside were two British-owned newspapers, and even they were censored. The little news of political significance they contained—including speeches criticizing the government in the Central legislature—was cut out before he received them (later he was allowed a few more papers and some books). To keep his sanity, he began to jot down stray thoughts and reactions to various news items in an exercise book he was allowed to keep. The first note was on the dissolution of the Comintern. It showed how far his disillusionment with the Soviet Union had gone, even compared to the views he had expressed after Hitler attacked it ("With all its faults, Soviet Russia is a giant fortress of world socialism and the proletariat"). Now he wrote: "The leaders of Russia had long given up the objectives of a World Revolution. The Comintern had already been converted merely into a Russian Fifth Column and had been acting as such....The disappearance of the Comintern did not imply the disappearance of the Fifth Column. Even when the Comintern lived and breathed, the various national communist parties were not so much under the control and supervision of the Comintern Secretariat as the agents of the Russian Secret Service. The latter held the whip not only over the national communist parties, but also over the Soviet embassies and consulates the world over."

A note dated 8 May 1944 on Gandhi's release from prison shows him torn between relief over the release in view of Gandhi's ill-health and concern lest this lead to a settlement during the war "because I believe that any settlement in the present conditions and on terms that these conditions will naturally determine, will do no good to the cause of India's freedom." By 11 August he was even more worried and sarcastic: "Violence it seems is a terrible sin, but only when used against British rule. For don't you see Mahatma Gandhi himself is straining his utmost to have a 'national government' established, at the command of which hundreds of thousands of Congressmen—the young ones, of course—will shoulder a gun and march forth in the shadow of fluttering tri-colours to murder and mutilate the brutal Jap and the bestial German....Gandhiji is a deadly dialectician, and there is no doubt he could make any intelligent person understand his logic. The trouble is I have no intelligence!"

On 5 August he was even more unhappy, but for quite another reason. "For many weeks now, since Gandhiji made his comments on the August movement a great bitterness has been growing in my heart....I feel bitter because I find we have been badly let down—not I personally, because I openly preached violence and was therefore prepared in the event of failure for severe censure and excommunication. But thousands, rather lakhs, of Indian patriots have been let down....I seem to remember the Congress President eloquently asking every Indian in such an event (the arrest of Congress leaders) to become his or her own leader. Is it fair, then, to disown those who did become their own leaders and followed the call of the Congress? Had they succeeded the Congress would have got the credit; when they failed should not the failure too be that of the Congress?"

Five days later he scribbled a note on communal unity: "The conflict is really between the national and communal forces in our national life. A settlement between the Congress and the Muslim League will not be a settlement between Hindus and Muslims, but between the national and communal ways of life." Then a comment on a theme that would recur. "My experience is that Congress committees devote the greater part of their time and energy to elections—Congress elections and elections to local bodies and provincial legislatures. It is my firm conviction that if the Congress gave itself say five years to an intensive preparation for a struggle through constructive and educative work among the masses, and introduced vigour and energy into its organization, it would be possible to launch a struggle that would sweep all opposition away and bring the British to their knees. I believe if this were done, and further if an understanding was reached with such bodies as the Muslim Majlis, we shall succeed in rallying a large section of the Muslim masses and intelligentsia under the banner of freedom and nationalism."

Then, on 1 September, another thought that would become familiar. "It seems to me that the basis of the entire social life of India, including political and economic life, was corporate and not individual. The corporate basis was finally destroyed by British rule and British individual conceptions. I believe that unless we reshape our life on the same old basis again, we shall fail to acquire the unity and strength of national life that we aim at."

The notes varied widely in language and content, reflecting the strain and loneliness of solitary confinement. On 25 October, when he was feeling isolated and depressed, he heard a knock on the cell door—"I rose and went up to the door, and whom did I see but Ram Manohar (Lohia), his eyes twinkling as ever through his glasses.....Was it a dream or magic? Yet, there he was, solid enough to be real though thinner somewhat. So things—real things that happen in the real world—happen in my cosmos too—even though they take thirteen months in happening. I wonder how long this illusion of reality will last."

Lohia had been able to evade arrest until May that year when he was captured in Bombay. After a month, he, too, was despatched to Lahore fort for intensive interrogation. What this meant was described by him subsequently in a letter to Harold Laski of the London School of Economics who was then chairman of the British Labour Party. "I would here indicate that I was ill-treated in one way or other for over four months," he wrote, "I was kept awake day after day, night after night, the longest single stretch running into ten days and that when I resisted the police in their efforts to make me stand, they wheeled me round on my manacled hands on the matted floor."

By the end of 1944, however, the tide of war had turned. With the Japanese being pushed out of Burma, there was no question any longer of India being invaded. Early in the new year, both JP and Lohia were moved to the relatively pleasant environment of Agra central jail. But since they were classed as violent revolutionaries and, more important, could be expected to oppose any compromise settlement with Britain, they were kept in prison until April 1946 while Nehru, Azad and other senior Congress leaders were released in June 1945 after the war had ended in Europe, and Japan was reduced to defending its home islands. Even the defeat of Japan two months later and the return of a Labour government to power in Britain did not lead to their release.

Meanwhile, Prabhavati had been arrested soon after returning to Patna from the Quit India session in August 1942, and had been detained without trial in Darbhanga Jail. In early 1944 Gandhi, who was being held at the Aga Khan's palace in Poona, had requested Lord Linlithgow to allow her to join him and act as a nurse for Kasturba, who was seriously ill. She was taken to Poona under heavy escort, where on 22 February

Kasturba died in her arms. Despite Gandhi's protests against the cruelty of taking her away from him at such a time, she was then sent back to Darbhanga and not released until early 1946.

But JP was far from forgotten. Friends and admirers made frequent attempts to secure his release. One of them, the Bombay lawyer H.R. Pardivala, even got himself imprisoned for two days when he filed a habeas corpus application on his behalf. After the other national leaders were released, the younger and more radical section of the Congress and students throughout the country kept up an incessant campaign demanding that he be set free.

CHAPTER EIGHT

BREAK WITH CONGRESS

When JP emerged from Agra central jail on 11 April 1946, his popularity was second only to Jawaharlal Nehru's, and even higher among students. He was feted all the way home to Patna, with large crowds turning out wherever he appeared. To some he symbolized the spirit of uncompromising resistance to foreign rule; others looked to him for a way past the constitutional and communal hurdles coming up in the path to freedom. He fitted the part. Tall, handsome, patently sincere, the long period of solitary confinement had enhanced the air of detachment from routine human desires and ambition. But he was not destined to play any part in the legalistic negotiations leading to the transfer of power from British to native hands. At the same time, the mass adulation he received would create a rift between him and other socialist leaders, especially Lohia, who did not regard himself inferior in any way.

The stage was already set for negotiations. The British cabinet mission had arrived in India on 23 March, 18 days before JP's release. Consisting of Lord Pethick-Lawrence, Sir Stafford Cripps and A.V. Alexander, its coming was interpreted as an indication that the new Labour government really meant to hand over power. But the Muslim League's demand for partition had also hardened. This and the future of the princely states became the main problems to be solved. For the rest, independence began to be seen exclusively in terms of taking over the reins of government from the British within a set constitutional framework, much as one party succeeds another if elected. The question of changing the style and values of the administration from colonial to democratic was forgotten.

Two days after his release JP met the mission while passing

through Delhi on his way home. He also saw the top Congress leaders, Azad, Nehru and Patel. But the meetings were a polite formality. He had already made his attitude clear to the press: that the country must be prepared to wage another mass struggle if the negotiations failed. He did not accept the thesis that the British Government was motivated by goodwill for India. In his view, the negotiations were "the result of the greatest national upheaval since 1857 and also of outside pressures and the world situation." Negotiations would have to be backed by mass sanctions if they were to be successful.

The crowd that gathered in Patna to celebrate the hero's homecoming would not be equalled for another 28 years, when he would return from voluntary exile from politics to inspire a mass movement. A Congress ministry had recently taken office after the first post-war general election. It was headed by Srikrishna Sinha, his old hostel mate, and it was he who presided over the huge public meeting. The noted Hindi poet Ramdhari Singh Dinkar recited a poem composed specially for the occasion.

But the enthusiastic reception and Sinha's presence did not prevent JP from expressing all the fears and doubts that had been welling up in prison about Congress policies. He justified the Quit India movement on the lines he had noted in Lahore fort and criticized the constitutionalist and parliamentary approach being taken currently by the Congress leaders. He again made the point that unless they prepared to launch another struggle if necessary, they would not get real independence.

At any time, the bulk of the leadership would not have relished such advice. Now there was no chance at all. They were tired, and hungry for the power and prestige of office, now that it seemed within grasp. The cabinet mission's visit was to prove fruitless. But the protracted negotiations made it pathetically obvious that the Congress leaders could be persuaded to compromise on basic issues, especially since Gandhi was no longer playing a leading role. The Muslim League came to realize that intransigence was the best strategy to achieve Pakistan, and the British Government, that the Congress might be pushed into a position of accepting partition.

The Congress leaders put their own interpretation on the part of the cabinet mission's plan concerning the setting up of a constituent assembly and accepted it. But the League had its own interpretation. It seized on a speech by Nehru to assert that the Congress was not sincere, pulled out of the plan, and threatened "direct action." This in turn led to the Great Calcutta Killings, the first of the series of communal massacres that would lead to partition.

When the cabinet mission plan was placed before the AICC at Bombay in July, JP was there to oppose it. To add a touch of drama, a sick Yusuf Meherally was brought in on a stretcher to contribute his opposition. JP took the stand that the cabinet mission plan was a manoeuver to persuade the Congress to swallow its principles and compromise with the League which was its ally. The real question before the country was not whether to accept the constituent assembley scheme but how to make use of the new spirit of nationalism that had now imbued even the armed forces and the police to achieve independence. JP carried his opposition to the decision to participate in the constituent assembly proposed by the cabinet mission to the extent of stopping CSP members from seeking election to it. The proposed assembly was far from the representative body elected under universal adult suffrage that the Congress had itself promised. Its members would be elected indirectly by the provincial assembles set up under the Act of 1935 which gave representation to no more than 15 per cent of the population. "There is only one course open to us," he told the AICC, "and that is to strengthen the Congress organization and when we are sure of our inherent strength, start a fight with the British Government, compel them to quit India and make them understand that they have to transfer power and that can be done only by negotiating with the Congress."

He felt strongly enough to put out a "third letter to the fighters of freedom" on 9 August 1946, the anniversay of the launching of the Quit India movement, on the model of the two he had written after his escape from Hazaribagh. Some of the fears he expressed concerning the consquences of Congress policy were overdrawn; for instance that the constituent assembly would not be able to declare India an independent republic. Some were understated. He anticipated the divisive character of a constitutionalist approach to independence, but did not actually warn against partition. But in several other respects, the letter itself anticipates his thinking nearly thirty years later when seeking to organize new forces to achieve social change.

He regretted, for instance, that "the Congress is becoming converted into a parliamentary party....A constitutional and administrative machinery might be of use in certain circumstances, but situated as we are, the people's struggle must be carried on mainly outside the legislatures and the portals of government departments....At the present moment the only manner we can wage this struggle is by forging mass sanctions. The creation of mass sanctions includes, first the psychological preparation of the masses for the struggle, second, the building up of organizations for the masses, such as peasant and labour unions, volunteer corps, student and youth organizations, village republics and weavers' cooperatives and myriad other organizations which would help in different ways to develop the collective strength and consciousness of the people....National unity cannot be imposed from above. It must be based on unity at the bottom."

And a few paragraphs later, a sentence that could have been written on the eve of the Bihar movement in 1974: "If the present Congress leadership persists in its attempt to transform the Congress into a mere parliamentary body with no constructive programme, relying entirely on governmental machinery to serve or rule over the people, turning more and more bureaucratic, keeping its hold over the Congress organization by the distribution of patronage and largesse, we shall no doubt be unavoidably drawn into conflcit with it."

In the same letter JP discussed the problem of working with the Congress when it was taking a line with which the socialists differed basically. "The official policy of the Congress today is not a policy of struggle or preparation for a struggle; it is rather a policy of compromise and constitutionalism. Therefore, it is not possible for us today who still adhere to the policy of struggle and revolutionary action to function in the name of the Congress." But he was not prepared to split the Congress at that point and still hoped that the organization could be used to bring about social change. "I am very clear in my mind that it would do the greatest possible injury to the cause of freedom in this country if we were to leave the Congress and form a parallel mass organization....The leadership is not identical with the organization....The Congress represents the greatest organized national and social force in the country and exercises unparalleled power over the mass mind. It would be foolish to give up this instrument as long as the possibility exists of its being utilized for a revolutionary purpose."

But the gap between JP and the Congress leadership continued to widen as it got more and more deeply enmeshed in the web of constitutional negotiations. As JP had feared, the Congress was pushed into the position of being one party to a disputed succession with the League as the other, and the British Government—an interested party—posing as mediator. The League held all the cards. Since it was the Congress that wanted the British to withdraw as soon as possible, the League had only to hold up the negotiations on one excuse or other to force the Congress to make further compromises. A gradual shift in the stand taken by the British Government also helped the League. Before the cabinet mission left for India, Prime Minister Attlee gave the assurance that while mindful of minority rights "we cannot allow a minority to place a veto on the advance of the majority." After the Congress had been involved fully in discussions on the complex, three-tier scheme (Centre, groups, provinces) plus a constituent assembly, proposed by the mission, and given a taste of power in an interim government, the British Government modified its stand. A new declaration on 6 December stated: "Should a constitution come to be framed by a constituent assembly in which a large section of the Indian population had not been represented, His Majesty's Government could not of course contemplate—as the Congress stated they would not contemplate—forcing such a constitution upon any unwilling parts of the country." The green signal for Pakistan was finally given on 20 February 1947, when Attlee said that his government had decided to transfer power not later than June 1948. But if a constitution had not been drafted by "a fully representative constituent assembly" by then, the British Government would decide whether to hand over power to a central government or in some areas to provincial governments." After this, it was not difficult to scrap the unwieldy cabinet mission proposals altogether and replace them with an attractively simple plan on paper: to transfer power to two dominions, one called India ruled by the Congress, the other called Pakistan ruled by the Muslim League. And to push it through even faster by appointing a dynamic, attractive but cold-blooded Lord Louis Mountbatten as the last Viceroy.

It was not only constitutional manoeuvres that won Pakistan for the League. Its trump card was to resort to "direct action" of extra-constitutional pressure by fomenting communal riots. It was helped in this by communal Hindu parties, and communalists in the Congress, who had as little interest in creating a secular India. The broad secular and reformist stream in the Congress, represented by Jawaharlal Nehru, was diverted into barren constitutional negotiations. As for Gandhi, his advice was no longer always acceptable to the Congress leadership and he devoted his last days to checking as much of the violence as he could by travelling through riot-stricken areas or fasting to bring communal leaders to their senses.

The threat of another mass movement suggested by JP and his socialist comrades was the only form of extra-constitutional pressure available to the Congress. But the Congress leadership was no longer willing to take the risk, with the possibility of a smooth transfer of the existing colonial administration to them apparently within sight. A successful mass movement could also generate unpredictable forces of social change, which the conservatives feared. Then there was the risk of mass violence, of virtual civil war, which made even Gandhi have second thoughts though he opposed partition to the end. In fact, as it happened, the unhealed wounds of partition would lead to much more death and destruction in the next 25 years than thay could have possibly imagined.

Side by side with his effort to divert the Congress from the path it was taking, JP continued to build up the Congress Socialist Party and infuse it with new ideas. He emerged from jail a convinced social democrat, eager to convert all his comrades, some of whom had come to the same conclusion much earlier. He addressed study circles and party meetings whenever he had time. He also wrote frequently in the party journal *Janata*. The model he envisaged was peculiarly Indian in many ways, providing the base for the gramdan structure he would build upon later under the influence of Acharya Vinoba Bhave.

The first conference of the Congress Socialist Party after the war was held in Kanpur towards the end of February 1947 and its proceedings reflected the new issues. With its leaders, especially JP and Achyut Patwardhan, having taken every opportunity to condemn the constitutionalist approach of Congress leaders to independence, relations with the parent party were strained. It

Break with Congress

was at this session that the party dropped the word "Congress" from its name and became just "Socialist Party." It also decided to go in for mass membership and not require its members to join the Congress as well. But on the advice of JP and Narendra Deva, the party decided not to sever its links with the Congress altogether. Although totally opposed to the consitutionalist path it was taking, they did not want to split nationalist force at a crucial time when partition of the country seemed a real possibility and communal riots were erupting in province after province. But this did not prevent JP from saying he had "no faith in the policy of compromise and negotiation which the Congress has been following of late. I have no faith in constitutional methods for vindicating our objectives and believe that they would weaken our movement for indepndence....If we had prepared for revolution instead of following constitutional means there would have been no internal weakness in our body politic."

On the ideological plane he stressed the contrast between democratic socialism and totalitarian communism, which he said it was wrong to call socialism. Under totalitarian communism, he told the conference, "every party but the ruling party is suppressed; no opposition is permitted to the government, i.e. to the bureaucracy in power; trade unions are not independent organizations of workers but subordinate limbs of the all-powerful State and the ruling party....The individual is not free and enjoys no protection against arbitrary loss of his already restricted freedom, his job or even his life. The State in such a system acquires an unchallenged control over the life, liberty and happiness of its subjects. On the other hand, thanks to the single-party system, the State passes entirely out of the democratic control of the community of workers and becomes a tool in the hands of the ruling clique of the only party in existence. Party leaders and the leaders of industry, agriculture and the armed forces become a class apart from the mass of workers, perpetuating themselves through a system of special privileges, drawing incomes far in excess of ordinary wages...."

On the other hand, "in the socialist society of our conception the individual, i.e. the worker, is free and the State has no power to deprive him of his rights and privileges except through due process of law. Further, in such a society the trade unions are free and may even exercise, if need be, their right to strike: other voluntary organizations of working men are also free; political parties other than the party in power may be formed and function freely. The State has no monopoly over the press, radio or other means of propaganda....In such a society, economic power, i.e. the power to plan production; the power to determine the conditions of work, prices, the distribution of **the national produce between saving and spending and between the forms and grades of these**—all these powers—are held not exclusively by the State bureaucracy, but shared by trade unions, cooperatives and other suitable representative bodies of working men.

"In such a society the servants of the State, particularly at the higher level, including police officers and magistrates, are elected by appropriate constituents and are subject to recall by the same. No incomes in such a society are much removed from the ordinary wage levels and the children of the higher grade of wage-earners have no special privileges or opportunities. Government and management of economic affairs are made as simple as possible, enabling immediate participation in these activities of the greatest possible part of the community."

After drawing this picture, however, he warned against making the mistakes of social democracy in Europe which had "allowed capitalism to re-entrench itself under the garb of democracy and constitutionalism." He advised the Socialist Party to "adhere steadfastly to the path of revolution" and saw no conflict between democracy and revolution.

His words had little impact on the course of events in India which were moving rapidly on two levels. On one, negotiations continued between the Viceroy and Congress and League leaders towards the inevitable goal of partition. There was an element of unreality about the talks because all concerned were aware of the outcome long before the plan was unveiled by Mountbatten on 3 June, ten weeks before it was put into effect. The socialists made their last stand at the AICC session called on 14-15 June to ratify Congress acceptance of the plan. It was a bitter debate. JP and Lohia clashed repeatedly with Nehru and Patel. At one point JP even suggested that Gandhi had not been kept fully informed about the negotiations when he was on his peace walk in East Bengal. But Gandhi did not want a breach on the eve of the transfer of power. Though still unhappy about the prospect of partition he did not challenge Nehru and Patel, and advised the socialists against launching the protest satyagraha they were considering. He insisted that unity was essential at such a time. When the time came to vote, therefore, the socialists abstained and the Mountbatten plan was approved by 153 to 29 with 36 abstentions.

Developments on the second level were only too real. JP saw the impact of communal frenzy on his home province when in October 1946 the Hindu majority turned on the Muslim minority in many parts of Bihar. The riots were ignited by reports of Muslim attacks on Hindus in Bengal. He did not conceal his revulsion. "It is clear from what I have been able to gather," he told the press, "that terrible and gruesome things have happened in Bihar, to the eternal shame of the province and of the majority community here. The Hindus of Bihar have been guilty of heinous crimes and have committed deeds of abject cowardice and barbarity...." He praised the interim government for putting down the riots firmly. On 3 November Nehru arrived in Patna with Patel and two Muslim members of his Interim Government. JP accompanied them on a tour of the worst affected districts. At Patna University, when students protesting against military firings to quell the riots shouted, "Nehru go back", he told them off and justified the shooting of murderers and looters, whom he described as traitors obstructing the path to freedom.

But JP never departed from the thesis that communal rioting was the result of a conspiracy between the Muslim League and the British Government, and that the Congress had fallen into the trap by going in for negotiations instead of mass agitations. Soon after his visit to Bihar he wrote an article in *Janata* headlined "Every Englishman a Leaguer." When the riots spread to Punjab in March 1947, he went there and said on his return: "The development of the recent events in the Punjab clearly indicates that the disturbances were carefully planned and were part of the conspiracy to instal the Muslim League in office as a step towards the final installation of Pakistan. Among other participants in this conspiracy were assuredly Governor Jenkins and his British colleagues in the province. It cannot be an accident that the districts where serious rioting broke out were precisely those districts which are ruled by British officers...."

On 14 and 15 August the British Raj was converted into two dominions, Pakistan and India. Among the few who did not join the celebrations were Gandhi and the socialists, and the first of the millions of refugees who would cross the new border in either direction

After the transfer of power there was little to hold the socialists in the Congress. They had developed divergent policies and attitudes. But the Nehru government was faced with such major problems in the first few months that JP and his colleagues accepted Gandhi's advice to not embarrass it. In September communal rioting came to Delhi; in October warfare with Pakistan began in Kashmir. In these circumstances, the new government could not be expected to reorganize straightaway the colonial system of administration it had inherited. But soon it became evident that it also accepted the style and values of the previous regime. The new rulers moved into the biggest houses vacated by senior British officials and in due course Prime Minister Nehru took over the walled-off palace of the British Commander-in-Chief (JP wrote him a letter criticizing the move). Gandhi's suggestion that the Congress convert itself into a social service organization was ignored. Shortly after the transfer of power JP wrote in an article: "The Congress has become a source of power and political advancement. Naturally, vested interests have grown and are fast growing within it, and with them corruption and jobbery. The Congress elections, beginning with enrolment of members, have become a racket and self-seeking and power politics have become rampant...."

All this brought JP and Gandhi closer together. They shared a concern for the exploited sections of society and a distaste for power politics that was becoming increasingly rare. When Acharya Kripalani resigned the office of Congress President, complaining that members of the new government did not consult him or keep him informed, Gandhi wanted JP to take his place. But Vallabhbhai Patel flatly refused to accept JP and Nehru tactfully suggested the name of the veteran socialist, Narendra Deva, who was less likely to gain mass support. Finally the choice fell on Rajendra Prasad, who was also president of the constituent assembly and hardly likely to rock the boat.

It was becoming increasingly difficult for the socialists to work within the Congress. Reports were coming in of their field workers in labour and peasant organizations being harassed by the police in Congress-governed provinces. Sometimes the socialists were themselves guilty of grave indiscipline in an effort to demonstrate their strength. One case that seriously upset the Congress leadership was when the socialists, under the guidance of Asoka Mehta, who had flowered into an outstanding trade union organizer, set up their own candidates for the Bombay Corporation elections and defeated those nominated by the Congress. Early in 1948, towards the end of January, JP met Gandhi and told him that the socialists could not stay in the Congress much longer. Gandhi said it would be difficult to function on their own, but no longer tried to dissuade him.

Next day, 30 January, Gandhi was dead, shot at point-blank range by a fanatic who resented his efforts, culminating in his recent fast, to secure communal harmony. A bomb had burst near his prayer meeting a few days earlier. Clearly there was a threat to his life. JP said what many people thought: that the government had been callously careless about giving him adequate protection and possibly this was because Home Minister Sardar Patel felt that his fast had denigrated the fledgling Government of India. Addressing a condolence meeting he said that the least that the government could do now was to drop the Home Minister, and thus antagonized Patel even more than he had already with his socialist views.

This was the last straw. Patel ran the Congress organization. Within a month the AICC passed a resolution amending the Congress constitution banning members of any party with a separate constitution (as the socialists had) from membership. In fact, Gandhi's death had removed the last bond between the Congress and the socialists. A month later, at Nasik, the socialists responded by quitting the Congress. The only province in which a sizable number decided to stay on in the Congress and leave the Socialist Party was UP. And, in contrast to standards set later, every socialist legislator who had been elected on the Congress ticket resigned his seat.

JP was general secretary of the Socialist Party when it took the historic decision to leave the Congress at Nasik on 19-21 March 1948. It was a landmark in his life, too, for he had been a Congressman since his return from the United States in 1929. His wide-ranging report to the session captured the importance of the occasion. It was a major document, describing and justi-

Break with Congress

fying the past record of the socialists and providing a significant glimpse of the direction his own thinking would take in the future. And it showed up a facet of his nature that had persisted since it had earned him the nickname "Baul" in his childhood and would continue. This was a lack of bitterness or rancour in his relations with persons however much he differed with their views; an innocent willingness to give the benefit of the doubt to his opponents unless evidence of duplicity was overwhelming. In the report he dwelt mainly on the constructive role an Opposition party could play in a democracy. There was need for a united front against the British before, but "now in a free India we must accustom the people to the idea that to be opposed to the Congress is not to be opposed to the nation, but rather to be opposed to certain policies and methods of government and to advocate alternative policies....There is much in common between the Congress and the Socialist Party: their faith in secular democracy brings them nearer together than any other two parties in the country. This naturally means that the Socialist Party shall ever be ready to fight for the defence of the state and of democracy and against the forces of communalism and reaction; and in this fight it would be happy always to join hands with the Congress.... I am conscious that when we leave the Congress we shall leave behind many friends and valued comrades with whom our bonds of personal and ideological attachment shell never snap."

Here he was obviously thinking primarily of Nehru who had written to him on the eve of the Nasik session. The letter illustrated the frank and informal relationship between them in spite of sharp differences on policy. Dated 15 March 1948, it began with "My dear Jayaprakash" and ended "Yours affectionately." It said: "You are meeting soon and are likely to take vital decisions. What you decide will naturally have an important effect on the country. You have sometimes discussed these matters with me in the past and I told you how I felt about them. I think the time has come when you must decide for yourself and no one else should seek to interfere with your decision. So I do not propose to say anything about it.

"But I should like, if I may, to express the hope that whatever the decision may be, it will be taken in a friendly spirit to others and with a desire to cooperate to the fullest extent possible. I know you feel this way and it is hardly necessary for me to stress this point. Still I am doing so as I feel the weight of our internal controversies greatly during this period of stress and trial. The internal situation is difficult enough, the external one is full of peril, and no one knows horror might not descend upon us before very long. So we must try our utmost to pull together and face these dangers together.

"With all good wishes."

The letter, however, did not prevent JP from stating his differences with Congress policy clearly and unambiguously. This was also necessary to satisfy a section in his party that was not too happy about leaving the Congress and giving up positions of influence and power. The CSP, he reminded them, had been formed as a reaction to the growth of what he called the "parliamentary mentality" in the Congress and to strengthen the organization "as an instrument of struggle." Then he went on to justify the negative stand the party had taken on the various British proposals. "The whole strategy of the Socialist Party and our reading of the situation," he explained, "were based on the assumption that the Congress would never accept partition. If partition had not been accepted, the Congress had no alternative but to resign from the Interim Government and face the British once again on the issue of full independence and an undivided India.... When the Congress accepted partition it accepted partial and not complete independence."

As for the constituent assembly, "As events developed and the Muslim League walked out of the Constituent Assembly, it was clear that what remained of that body was no longer capable of drafting the constitution of free India. The only thing that remained to be done then was, as I have said above, to tear up the whole agreement with the British, to get out of the Interim Government and of the constituent assembly, and to call finally a real constituent assembly elected by the people.... We were told that such a course of action would have led to civil war, which the acceptance of Pakistan would avoid. We replied that in the first place the risk should be taken, and in the second place, acceptance of Pakistan would not remove but accentuate that risk. Easily gained power however was too much of a temptation to be resisted, with what tragic results history has already shown."

Some of the points he made against the ruling party would be heard again: It had so identified itself with government that it had lost the power to protect the people. In fact they were saying: "The British have gone; the ICS have come." All India Radio was being used for party ends. Administrative authority was being used to curb the activities of opposition and trade union workers. Public safety acts were being misused to put down political rivals.

But the most significant section of the report dealt with the close relationship between ends and means, reflecting how far he had moved from orthodox Marxism and how near to Gandhi. The following is an extract:

"From time immemorial there have been politicians who have preached that there is no such thing as ethics in politics. In the old times, however, this amoralism did not spread it scorrupting influence beyond a small class that played at politics, and the mass of the people were left uncorrupted by what the leaders and ministers of State did. But since the rise of totalitarianism, which includes both Fascism-Nazism and Stalinism, this principle has been applied on a mass scale and every individual in society has been affected by it. This has resulted in such an eclipse of moral values from social life that not only its political sector has been darkened but every sector of human life, including even family life.

"Since the victory of Stalinist methods in Russia, it has been commonly believed that there is no room for moral values in Marxism, and it is usual for a socialist who talks of such matters to be branded as a renegade or, at the least, a deviationist. I should, therefore, like to state before you in the clearest possible terms that I for one have come to believe that for the achievement of socialism a strict regard for means is of the highest importance. Socialism means different things to different persons, but if by socialism we mean a form of society in which the individual is a cultured, a civilised being, is free and brave, kind and generous, then I am absolutely clear that we will never reach this goal except by strict adherence to certain human values and standards of conduct. It is too often believed that all would be well only if there were no exploitation in society and everyone was well fed and clothed and housed. But a society of well fed and clothed and housed brutes is a far cry from socialism.

"There were many things that Mahatma Gandhi taught us. But the greatest thing he taught us was that means are ends, that evil means can never lead to good ends and that fair ends require fair means. Some of us have been sceptical of this truth, but recent world events and events at home have convinced me that nothing but good means will enable us to reach the goal of a good society, which is socialism....

"There is a view held by some that all politics are power politics. I consider this to be a disastrous point of view. I shall examine here two important aspects of this way of thinking. First, let us see how it affects party organization. Those who hold this view should logically make every attempt—I do not say that they are actually doing so—to secure power within the party itself. And power, according to this view, being the quintessence of politics, the use of every kind of means may be considered justified to secure it, including means such as lying, scandal-mongering and cheating at party elections. Clearly—and I hope all of us would agree—such means could only result in the complete disintegration of the party. I, therefore, hope and pray that every one of us will reject all such means and eschew all quest for power within the party. It is human to yearn for recognition and aspire for positions of influence and leadership. But one should be content to reach these positions by virtue of one's work and service done to the cause.

"The second aspect of this view which I wish to examine here has far deeper and wider significance. The theory that all politics are power politics has the necessary underlying basis—though this may not be obvious to the protagonists of this theory—that the State is the only instrument of social good. In other words, those who subscribe to this theory believe—unless they are mere self-seekers, in which case unworthy of notice—that they must capture the State in order to be able to serve society and bring about the social transformation they desire.

"I reject this view completely. The Congress today has captured the State, but every thinking Congressman will agree that the Congress would completely undermine itself if it depended on the State for every effort at social change and development. In fact the view is growing among the constructive workers in the Congress that they must cut themselves off from the parliamentary machine and function independently so as to serve both society and the State.

"The experience of totalitarian countries, whether fascist or communist, has shown that if the State is looked upon as the sole agent of social reconstruction, we get nothing but a regimented society in which the State is all-powerful and popular initiative is extinct and the individual is made a cog in a vast inhuman machine. Such a society is surely not the objective of our party; nor could a society of the nature ever be an intermediate stage in the evolution of this democratic socialist society that is our aim.

"Democracy requires that the people should depend as little as possible on the State. And, both according to Mahatma Gandhi and Karl Marx, the highest stage of democracy is that in which the State has withered away. Totalitarianism, as distinct from a transitional 'dictatorship' of millions of toilers over a small defeated class of vested interests, can hardly be a half-way house to full democracy that popular effort has the freest possible chance and that the people, through varied kinds of economic and cultural organizations and institutions, are enabled and encouraged to improve their condition and manage their affairs.

"Accordingly, the type of mind that I should like to see develop within the Party is one that would make every one of us indifferent to whether one is Prime Minister of the Republic or a trade union or other field worker. I believe that whether or not we have the government in our hands, if we succeed by constructive work in creating a sound trade union movement capable of running industry; in educating the working class in the arts of citizenship; in creating cooperative communities in the villages; in mobilising the youth and children as voluntary servants of the nation; in creating cultural influences that go down even to the most backward sections of the people; if we succeed in eradicating superstition and bigotry; if we succeed in enlisting the cooperating of hundreds of thousands selfless workers to whom the seats of power offer no attraction—if we succeed in all this, we shall also succeed in building up a socialist society. In this event, the State will inevitably become a socialist State and will play its inevitable and appointed role, which would go little beyond the imprimatur of the law on what has already been accomplished, or on what cannot be prevented from happening. The State in this manner will only be an instrument in the hands of a popular socialist movement—i.e., of the people organized independently of the State for a socialist way of living—rather than the source and fountain-head of all authority and will.

"These observations are of particular significance in the context of the historic decision we are about to take. The temptation for members of an opposition party to look always to the seats of power is great. We must keep this temptation in check. We must remember today, and never forget it in the coming years, that it would be by constructive work rather than by the tactics of a parliamentary opposition, by positive service rather than by exploiting the mistakes and faults of others, that we would succeed in establishing a democratic socialist society."

CHAPTER NINE

STRAINS AMONG SOCIALISTS

An unintended consequence of the Socialist Party's resolve to go it alone was to bring out differences between its leaders that would eventually become unbridgeable. This in turn would be one of the main factors persuading JP to leave party politics altogether. On the surface the differences were on questions of policy and tactics. But personal rivalry and envy provided the motivation. The main protagonists were JP and Lohia, though on the level of ideology it was party theoretician Asoka Mehta who was initially attacked by the Lohia group. A thesis by him provided one of the major issues on which the party split.

Unwittingly, JP contributed to the friction. He was a natural leader and began to take his leadership for granted, often overlooking the need to consult colleagues before taking major decisions, such as adding communists to the CSP executive or boycotting the constituent assembly. Being transparently sincere himself, he failed to comprehend the emotions and grievances bottled up in others. Lohia was the one most affected. Intellectually, he was JP's equal and had gone through as much in the struggle for independence. But he was short, dark and wore thick spectacles. The crowds that gathered to greet the Quit India heroes showered their praise on JP, overlooking him. And JP did not make a point of involving him in discussions or receptions. Possibly as a defence mechanism, Lohia developed a caustic, wounding style of conversation, though he was generous in deed. This, too, upset JP who never engaged in personal innuendo. On the other hand, Lohia probably grew to resent his other-wordly moralistic tone.

It did not take long after Nasik for the differences to surface. The party held a study camp at Mahabaleshwar towards the end of October 1948 and it was here that they took contrary positions on an issue that would separate them completely—the attitude that the socialists should adopt towards the Congress, and Nehru in particular. JP felt, as he had said at Nasik, that they should take a soft, responsive line with the Congress and in any case be more concerned with field work than with capturing positions of power. But Lohia, a supreme rationalist who had earlier been reluctant to leave the Congress, now felt that since the socialists had formed a separate Opposition party, their main business should be to oppose and try to displace the Congress from office. He argued that although Nehru was a socialist in the realm of ideas, he was power-oriented and used other people to create the balance of forces required for his own survival. The obvious target of this remark was JP who did not doubt Nehru's sincerity or his goodwill towards the socialists. Many of JP's comrades however believed that Nehru made use of JP and the socialists only to counterbalance the conservative group headed by Patel.

Before the Mahabaleshwar camp, Nehru had written to JP expressing distress over "the wide gap which is ever growing between many of us and the Socialist Party." He went on to confess that "I cannot, by sheer force of circumstances, do everything that I would like to do. We are all of us in some measure prisoners of fate and circumstances. But I am as keen as ever to go in a particular direction and carry the country with me and I do hope that in doing so I would have some help from you...." This was just the kind of appeal that JP could not ignore.

JP spent most of his time touring the country. In fact, Nehru had complained in his letter "I have no idea where you are. Occasionally I read some report of your speech in some far corner of India." He was trying to strengthen the party organization and extend its influence in the trade union movement. He was already president of three major national unions—of railwaymen, post and telegraph workers and ordnance factory workers. In between, he had also sought votes for the new party in several by-elections, but the results were ominous. Even Acharya Narendra Deva was defeated in UP. Popularity was not so easily translatable into votes.

An entry in Prabhavati's diary during this period provides a glimpse of the hectic pace of JP's tours. On one trip they covered 550 miles by road, spent 60 hours in trains, attended 30 meetings; he made 40 speeches and collected Rs 20,811 for the party. He also turned out a steady stream of articles, letters and statements. He wrote to Rajendra Prasad, who was president of the constituent assembly, asking him to dissolve the assembly because it had been elected before partition on a very restricted franchise and was therefore unrepresentative; and convene a new one elected on the basis of adult franchise. He issued an angry statement when Lohia was arrested in May 1949 for demonstrating in front of the Nepalese Embassy in New Delhi in which he said: "There are more restrictions on the liberties of the citizen in free India today under Congress rule than there ever were under the worst British despots."

When Lohia was convicted, he prepared a second statement, which made the point that "for those dissatisfied with the present government there are two courses open. One that is followed by the communists, namely the path of chaos and anarchy; the other the path of democratic opposition, including the method of satyagraha and other forms of peaceful resistance to evil. In the interest of the country, the Socialist Party has deliberately chosen the second path."

If the national interest was clearly involved, however, he did not hesitate to cooperate with the ruling party, as he had promised at Nasik. When the situation began to heat up in the former princely state of Hyderabad in 1948 following clashes between the diehard Razakars and the local population, he toured its borders and addressed joint Congress-Socialist Party meetings in which he exhorted the Muslims of Hyderabad to resist the Nizam. He was able to carry conviction because his own commitment to secularism was above doubt.

The annual conferences of the Socialist Party provided occasions for JP to return to the theme of democratic socialism. At the Patna session in early March 1949, the central theme of his report was that socialism did not only have an economic content. There could be "no real socialism without enlargement of our liberty and freedom." Marx and Lenin both had said that democracy and socialism were inseparable, but their teachings had been distorted. "Democratic socialism must become our life's mission" and this "involved acceptance of democratic means, peaceful methods and constructive approach." The party constitution was revised to accord with these new principles. Selective membership on the communist pattern was abandoned and a mass membership campaign begun. Provision was also made for collective affiliation of trade unions, kisan panchayats and other mass organisations.

JP was more and more antagonized by communist tactics. He told the session: "The communists do not believe in truth. They had no honesty, no integrity. To them left unity is merely a manoeuvre, a device for acquiring a mass base by boring in from within other parties and organizations."

He returned to the theme at the next party conference in Madras in July 1950. But here he had to deal with a close colleague whose disgust with power politics exceeded his own. Achyut Patwardhan, one of the Quit India heroes, had sent in a letter expressing his desire to quit political work. The language was as eloquent as JP's own: "The effectiveness of ideology and the strength of an organization are at present judged by the simple test of attaining power as soon as possible. The inevitable result of this quest for political power is the growing vogue of ruthlessness in our public life. . . . In this perspective, social changes are treated as a function of the compulsive authority of the State. The movement of men's minds and the quickening of human sentiment are ignored and even come to be viewed as the results rather than the prime cause and source of all political authority...."

This was farther than JP was willing to go at this point. He remarked: "It is not possible for a political organization to convert itself into a spiritual organization, but as I have stated, the Socialist Party by subscribing to the principles of democratic socialism is endeavouring to safeguard those very human values which he (Achyut) wants to preserve by other means....It is precisely because we are interested in building up a socialist society and not a socialist state that we have raised the banner of democratic socialism."

However, the debate that followed showed that a section of the party felt that not only Achyut but JP as well was in danger of losing touch with political reality. A delegate from Orissa described JP's report as "singularly remarkable for its vagueness," and asked: "Was it not on account of such utopian conceptions that social democracy failed in Europe?" Another was unhappy with his "pedantic Gandhian manner." He complained that he had not suggested any real remedies. Those believing in violent insurrection were not convinced. A delegate from Bengal argued that insurrectionary methods were democratic if they had the backing of the people.

Before the session ended, it adopted a "programme for national revival." This mainly consisted of known socialist objectives like reducing the gap between rich and poor, village reconstruction and social integration. But even then there was a mention of black money and the document also stated: "The one greatest single enemy of the nation today is the evil of corruption."

After the Madras session, preparations for the first general elections to be held in the winter of 1951-52 dominated the thinking of the Socialist Party. Struggle and mass agitation took second place. On 19 May 1950, JP wrote to Nehru about a complaint that would be heard again and again: "You are perhaps aware of the doubts raised in opposition circles as to whether the coming general elections would be free and fair...."

I have heard that it is common talk in high Congress circles that no means would be spared to ensure a Congress victory. The complete and precipitous fall from Gandhian ideals of the Congress rather confirms one's doubts." He went on to complain of ministerial pressure being exerted on all concerned in a recent by-election in Bihar. "District magistrates, deputy commissioners and education and police officers were used to canvas and to collect ballot papers from the voters. Ministers, including the chief minister, personally telephoned to government servants advising them to vote for the Congress candidate."

Nehru replied in four days: "Government servants should not be used for party purposes. Ministers should bring no pressure on government servants. ... While this is quite clear, obviously some difficulties might well arise. Ministers are no doubt interested in elections and are members of a party. They are bound to participate in the elections and to some extent it may be difficult to distinguish between their individual and ministerial capacities. We are in the early stages of large scale elections. We have not yet developed the conventions and habits of mind which, say, a country like England has achieved through long course of years. ... I shall certainly draw the attention of all provincial governments to this question of governmental interference in elections."

The Socialist Party was hoping to do quite well and tried to reach electoral agreements with other Opposition parties with similar views. One such was the Democratic Congress, a Gandhian group which had broken away from the Congress under the leadership of Kripalani. Soon after the break, JP wrote to Kripalani saying: "I feel even now that if the Gandhians and the democratic socialists were to work together the course of history in this country might effectively be turned." The Democratic Congress soon joined hands with another group to form the Kisan Mazdoor Praja Party (KMPP). They did not respond too enthusiastically to JP's initiative at first, but the initiative would result in a merger in course of time.

JP's efforts were limited to electoral strategy and trying to ensure free and fair elections. He was not interested in standing for office (an attitude that has been consistent throughout his life) and expressed strong disagreement with the PSP national executive when it suggested that all prominent members of the party should contest the coming elections. "To me this question is of vital importance to the growth of the party and the future of democratic socialism," he wrote to the executive, "State power and initiative are not the only means of building up a democratic society but popular initiative and day-to-day effort are also essential; indeed the latter are ultimately more important....If both activities are of equal importance, why should all the important men be sent to the legislatures....If all the important men are sent to the legislatures, the task of building up the popular bases and sanctions of socialism (except as agitational appendages to parliamentary work) would be relegated to secondary place...."

The election results came as a great disappointment to the socialist leadership. Though they secured the second highest number of votes they won only 12 seats in the Lok Sabha, whereas the Communist Party, which had received about one-third as many votes, won 23 seats. The reason was that the socialist votes were thinly spread over the country but the communist vote was concentrated in a few areas.

Much of the blame for the disppointing election result fell on JP. In April, Ramanandan Misra, an old comrade with whom he had escaped from Hazaribagh jail, circulated a note to the Bihar unit of the party saying that JP was responsible because he discouraged revolutionary militancy and was on good terms with the Congress. JP was so upset that tears came to his eyes and he left the place.

Lohia was relatively restrained at the Pachmarhi conference of the Socialist Party in May 1952. As chairman of the session (in the absence of Narendra Deva), he did not blame any individual but made the point that the party "must definitely abandon its facing-both-ways policy in doctrine as well as in programmes. It should never be an auxiliary team of the Congress Party nor should it ever act as the sappers and miners of the Communist Party." This was the beginning of his theory of equidistance between Congress and communists which he developed as the correct line for the Socialist Party.

JP did not object to Lohia's speech. In fact he praised it. But he was very much on the defensive about his own role. He accepted responsibility for the policy and programme of the party but insisted that they were not responsible for its electoral reverses. Replying to those, like Ramanandan Misra, who maintained that the party had not involved itself adequately in mass struggle and agitation, he pointed to the unwisdom of launching countrywide movements after the nation had been shaken by partition and Gandhi's death. Local campaigns had been waged, many by Lohia. He had not been able to do much in this field himself "because you have burdened me with other responsibilities and tasks." The party might have done better if it had concentrated on a few areas, he said, as the communists had done, but then they would not have a national image. In his view, the main failing had been lack of hard, constructive work. The division of the opposition vote among a number of parties was another factor.

Orthodox socialists could not be blamed for feeling that JP was straying from the accepted path. A year earlier, he had welcomed the sarvodaya programme of national reconstruction with its emphasis on cooperation and decentralization, objectives he had himself put forward at Nasik. Significantly, in view of developments more than twenty years later, he also suggested that socialist and sarvodaya workers unite to create a social order based on the sarvodaya programme. Now at Pachmarhi, he referred to the bhoodan yagna campaign started by Vinoba Bhave as a major step in mobilizing public opinion in favour of land redistribution. This was in spite of the fact that, in strict Marxist terms, Vinoba favoured a process of class conciliation rather than conflict. But JP assuaged critics by saying that Vinoba was thinking of launching a nationwide satyagraha movement in two years if the government failed to redistribute land. (Vinoba's reluctance to contemplate any such step was responsible for JP's disenchantment with his approach to bhoodan years later.)

In June 1952 JP undertook a three-week fast in Poona. He felt he had let down the post and telegraph workers because he conveyed certain government assurances to them which had not been fulfilled concerning a strike. Conceding that he may have misunderstood the government's intentions, he felt he should go on a "self-purificatory fast" on the Gandhian model. (The identification had become very close after Gandhi's death. He had even started spinning—which he had ridiculed so much earlier—and attending prayer meetings with Prabhavati.) He emerged from the fast weak (having lost 17 pounds in weight) and more convinced than ever of the role of ethical concepts like goodness in improving human society. This was when he finally rejected the Marxist concept of dialectical materialism—as he explained in an article in *Freedom First*—because a materialist philosophy could not accommodate the non-material urge to acquire and practise goodness which was at the heart of human progress. He amplified these ideas before a wider audience in an address to the First Asian Socialist Conference in Rangoon in January 1953.

The dissident Congressmen and others who had banded together in the KMPP were even more disappointed than the socialists by the election results. This made them more amenable to the idea of cooperation with the Socialist Party. In fact, the discussions went so well that both parties resolved to merge into one—the Praja Socialist Party (PSP) in September 1952. This made good sense because the KMPP had a following in areas in which the socialists were weak. Most of the leaders of the KMPP had been Gandhians, and this fitted quite well into the sarvodaya tilt given to the Socialist Party by JP. Acharya Kripalani was appointed chairman of the new party. Welcoming the union, he stressed the basic identity between the merging parties. "We both want a classless and casteless society free from social, political and economic exploitation. The socialists call it the socialist society. We call it the Sarvodaya society." Asoka Mehta, who was made general secretary, said that the merger would end the dangerous polarization in the public mind between the Congress and the communists.

But the rejoicing was shortlived. Differences on the attitude to be taken towards the Congress and, more specifically, Nehru, which had been submerged in the rush of events after the Mahabaleshwar camp, now re-emerged stronger than ever. Despite sharp differences between them, JP and Nehru had kept in touch. The death of Sardar Patel in December 1950 had removed an obstacle between them. Patel had developed an obsessive dislike for JP, which he expressed in a letter to Nehru in June 1948: "I have all along been of the view that if the future of India is in the hands of men like Jayaprakash, it would probably be a most unfortunate circumstance...." Late in 1952, Nehru felt strong enough to seek closer relations with the PSP to counterbalance the remaining conservatives in his party. He held a series of meetings with JP, Kripalani and Narendra Deva on the possibility of their joining the Union Government and some of their colleagues joining state governments in areas in which the PSP was strong. But the talks were infructuous. The break came in March 1953 when the correspondence between Nehru and JP was released.

The correspondence did not disclose much that was not known. The main reason for publishing it was to squelch rumours circulated largely by Lohia's group to sabotage the talks. The letters, accompanied by explanatory notes by JP and Nehru were designed to set the record straight. The actual discussions took place verbally.

JP's letter was written on 4 March 1953 after the talks had begun. It included a 14-point draft policy programme. It was both friendly and hard-hitting. The form of address was still "My dear Bhai," but it started with saying that the Prime Minister was "out of touch with what we (the PSP) have been doing or saying or thinking." Later he added: "You seem to have been unduly impressed with the chits that foreigners have given your government." But about Nehru's initiative to PSP, he said: "The proposal that you made to me was a bold and unusual one because the Congress Party stood in no need of a coalition either at the Centre or in most of the States. But you rose above partisan considerations and took a statesmanlike step. What you proposed was, to my mind, not a parliamentary coalition in the accepted sense of the term, but a joint effort to build a new India. We are not a power in the legislatures, but we do claim to have a following in the country and a cadre which in some respects is superior to that of the Congress.... A great deal would depend on how you conceived your own move in asking for our cooperation. If it means only that a few of us are to be added to your cabinet and some to the state cabinets to strengthen the government and your hands in carrying out your present policies, the attempt would not be worth making. But if it means launching upon a bold, joint venture of national reconstruction, it might well have been a historic move.... It is in this perspective that the draft programme was prepared."

Another point to which JP drew Nehru's attention was that "China and India are the two countries in Asia to which all Asia and Africa are looking. If India fails to present anything but a pale picture of a welfare state.... I am afraid the appeal of China would become irresistible and that would affect the lives of millions and change the course of history disastrously."

Among the points on which he laid special stress were devolution of power and decentralization of authority, effective machinery against corruption, and reforms in the legal system.

After explaining some of the proposals, he said that if this basis of cooperation was not acceptable to Nehru the idea could be dropped, and "as there has been much public speculation over this subject, you might state on an appropriate occasion that you had certain talks with us regarding cooperation, but the talks did not reveal a common approach to the country's problems and so they were discontinued."

The 14-point programme that JP sent to Nehru with his letter included:

1. Amendments to the Constitution
   (a) to remove obstacles in the way of social change;
   (b) to abolish guarantees to princes, and civil servants, etc.
   (c) to abolish second chambers.
2. (a) Administrative reforms at all levels, including decentralization of political power and administrative authority;
   (b) reform of law and legal procedure;
   (c) summary and effective machinery to deal with corruption.
3. (a) Redrawing the administrative map of India on the basis of linguistic, economic and administrative considerations. Appointment of a commission by the parliament to work out the details on the basis of the above mentioned principles;
   (b) reduction of administrative costs by having regional (multistate) governors, High Courts, and other top level tribunals and public service commissions.
4. (a) Redistribution of land to remove economic inequality and exploitation; preference to be given in all such schemes to landless labour and poor peasants;
   (b) immediate stoppage of all evictions;
   (c) suitable legislation to prevent fragmentation and bring about consolidation of holdings;

(d) abolition of the remaining forms of landlordism;
(e) rural economy to be transformed into a cooperative economy through compulsory multi-purpose societies;
(f) state assistance in providing credit and other facilities to agriculture; such assistance to be given through multipurpose societies;
(g) the State, as far as possible, to deal not with individual peasants but through a group of them organized in a cooperative or panchayat. This should include collection of land revenue, a part of which to remain with the village as organized in the multipurpose society of panchayat.

5. Reclamation of waste lands and settlement of landless labour on them through village collectives. No wastelands to be allotted for capitalist farming.
6. Nationalization of banks and insurance companies.
7. Progressive development of state trading.
8. Selected number of plants in different industries to be owned and run by the state cooperatives or autonomous corporations or workers' councils. Fostering organizations of technicians and managers to provide expert advice and administrative personnel for state enterprises.
9. Unified trade union movement organized on the basis of the union shop. This will enable the unions to become socially responsible agencies.
10. Nationalization of coal and other mines producing important minerals.
11. Association of workers in the management of state enterprises.
12. Demarcation of spheres of large and small-scale industries, and establishing, encouraging and protecting small-scale industries.
13. As a first step towards achieving economic equality in the country higher salaries and emoluments in governmet

services shall be scaled down.
14. The spirit of swadeshi to be promoted and made to pervade all walks of life.

Nehru replied on 17 March:

My dear Jayaprakash,

I received your letter of the 4th March from Gaya some days ago. I did not reply to it as you were coming to Delhi and yesterday we had a talk...

My own purpose in having talks with you, as well as with Kripalaniji and Narendra Deva, was to bring about as large a measure of cooperation in our activities as possible. Also to infuse that very sense of urgency, as well as clarification of our goals. You will remember that I have been trying to meet you for many months past. This was no new urge due to any new occurrence. Long before you undertook your fast, I wrote to you and suggested that you might see me. But this could not be arranged, because of your fast and subsequent convalescence. Thus my desire to discuss these matters with you was not related to any new happening, but had been present in my mind for a long time past. It was obviously due to a feeling that we have big things to do in this country and we should approach them with our joint effort. I feel the next five or ten years are crucial in our existence. I am not satisfied, if I may say so, with the rate of our progress or advance. I wanted to hasten it and I wanted your help to do so.

I did not think of any precise method of doing so. It was rather the general approach that mattered. I had not thought of, what is called, merger of parties. I felt that if there was a mutual realisation of the necessity of cooperation, other things would flow from it. When you or Kripalaniji asked me for greater precision, I said that I was prepared to consider this question at all levels, including both popular and governmental. It was left at that and we did not discuss this particular matter any further.

Our talks have resulted in a good deal of speculative publicity, much of it wide of the mark. That should be cleared, though it is never possible to prevent people from giving vent to their own thoughts.

I feel after reading your letter and after my talk with you that, perhaps, any kind of a formal step at the present moment would not be helpful. We have to grow into things, not to bring them about artificially. You have sent me a draft programme which includes among other things, basic constitutional changes. Now, obviously, it is not easy for me to bring about these changes, even though I may not be opposed to them. You refer to all kinds of other changes of law and legal procedure and administration and reorganisation of the map of India, etc. To each one of these, considered separately, I have little objection and I would be happy to give thought to them. But, surely, it is beyond me both as Prime Minister and as the President of the Congress to deal with such vital matters and give assurances in regard to them. Many of these may be logically justifiable and yet there may be other reasons which come in the way. Again, one can hardly take all these things in a bunch.

At the same time, from your point of view, you are perfectly justified in putting forward what you consider the immediate programme to be.

There lies the difficulty, and it is because of this that I feel that it is better for us not in any way to tie each other down, but rather to try to the best of our ability, to develop both the spirit and the practice of cooperation. I am quite sure that this is possible over a large field. That should not come in the way of your pursuing your particular aims and objectives or pressing for any changes in our programme. It is the spirit and the approach that count. If that spirit and approach are there, then we will influence each other in our policies and gradually come nearer. At a later stage we might be able to take further steps towards closer cooperation.

I agree with you, therefore, that for the present we should drop this idea in its more precise forms and make this clear to the public in as friendly a way as possible in order to put an end to public speculation.

I do hope that we shall meet frequently to discuss common problems, and there are so many of them, and try to help each other to understand them fully. Certainly, I would welcome your help, as well as Kripalaniji's and Narendra Deva's. Indeed, perhaps, it might be better to do so without being tied down to any particular approach or formula.

Yours affectionately,
JAWAHARLAL

Thus the parting was polite, with each leader trying to make things easier for the other. But such cordiality only heightened Lohia's suspicions that JP was willing to give up the path of struggle in return for a senior ministerial position and the unwritten assurance that he would succeed Nehru as Prime Minister. He used every available forum to campaign against the move, often speaking in harsh language. But the essence of his argument was based on a principle that JP would himself accept later. This was that a change at the top was ineffectual unless it represented a shift in opinion at the grassroots. Mobilization of mass opinion must have priority.

Writing in *Janata* in May 1953 he explained the core of his argument: "There are two ways in which Shri Narayan may succeed Shri Nehru. One of these ways is through the benevolent goodwill and agreement of Shri Nehru and that way people like me will resist to the utmost of our capacity, for Shri Narayan in such case would prove to be a worse prime minister than Shri Nehru. The other way is that of being allowed to appear at the head of the tens of milions of people voting for socialism or acting in massive civil disobedience. This way people, I think, will assist with the utmost of their strength. In this case Jayaprakash Narayan will prove a better prime minister."

The difference came to a head in the same month when the PSP held its first convention at Betul in Madhya Pradesh. The explosive charge was contributed by Asoka Mehta, who was general secretary, in a thesis entitled "Political Compulsions of a Backward Economy." He argued that some measure of cooperation with the government on economic development was essential in a poor and backward country. Otherwise, economic problems would push the country towards totalitarianism or make the government too timid to pursue big plans. One way to resolve the dilemma was to give the government a broader base by involving other parties, but in an institutional framework not on an *ad hoc* basis. Coming soon after the infructuous talks between JP and Nehru, this made many delegates feel that a merger was still on the cards. The majority of delegates strongly criticized Mehta's thesis as well as any effort to move closer to the Congress

Lohia returned to his thesis that the PSP should be equidistant from the Congress and the communists. He then went on to ridicule the sarvodaya plan for cooperative rather than competitive politics in which political parties would have no place—or partyless democracy in JP's terminology. "A no-party or an all-party effort inevitably leads to either some kind of dictatorship or to the building of a political party of one's choice. I can well understand the effort to remove the difficulties and weaknesses of a party, but I cannot understand the decrying of the party system altogether."

Another point he made condemned not only the Mehta thesis but also anyone who supported it. This was typical of the sweeping indictments he often made. "Far more dangerous than the actual achievement of cooperation or coalition is the attitude of mind it generates. The search for areas of agreement somewhat removes from sight the very much wider areas of disagreement. In a country where 100 million people have to live on one meal a day, where near-famine stalks from state to state and full famine is threatened, where ejectments, police repression, unemployment and other injustices continuously prevail, the party will only stultify itself by shutting its eyes to the sweeping areas of disagreement with the ruling party."

JP was again on the defensive, admitting that "the entire criticism was directed against me. The debate so far has centred round my talk with Mr Nehru." He described Mehta's thesis as a device to shield him. Describing his talks with Nehru, he said that Kripalani, Narendra Deva and Lohia had all opposed the idea of cooperating with the Congress. It was Nehru who had taken the initiative and it was he who ended the talks. Asked for an assurance that the talks would not be resumed, he said: "Even while I still hold that, given the necessary goodwill and agreement, the joint effort I was visualising is desirable and appears to be the only way to face and solve the tremendous problems of economic development and national integration facing the country today. I will have no further talks with Mr Nehru on the question."

On the subject of multi-party democracy that had attracted criticism from Lohia, he described his comments as loud thinking, but went on to say: "I have come to believe that the party system will not be conducive to national integration. It is an unsatisfactory system and is incapable of providing an adequate framework for the democratic requirements of the masses. As a result talent gets divided, national effort gets split and it leads to the imposition of a majority view." He had no alternative to offer, but was mentioning the subject in an effort to get people to think about it. The rest of his speech was focused on the virtues of bhoodan.

The same evening (15 June) JP sent in his resignation from the national executive of the party, suggesting that those "opposed to cooperation with the Congress come forward and take up organisational responsibilities." Mehta and the three joint secretaries joined him. But Lohia avoided a breach by making what he himself described as his shortest speech: "On behalf of the convention I request my esteemed colleagues to continue."

At the next meeting, Lohia went even further to patch up relations. "Jayaprakash and I, what else can I say about our relationship except that in the past we have both faced bullets together. It is another matter that no bullets hit us. Beyond saying that I have had no brother of my own, it is unnecessary to say anything more....Asoka (Mehta) and I have in the past talked till early hours of the morning and we could not be talking just politics at that hour."

Camaraderie and shared suffering enabled the old CSP team to overcome suspicion and envy for the time being, but difference surfaced again. The question of relations with other parties came up in a specific form in 1954. When elections were announced in Travancore-Cochin (later Kerala), the PSP negotiated an electoral alliance with the communists with the objective of preventing a Congress majority. No party emerged with a clear majority and in a bid to stop the communists from forming a government, the Congress offered to support a PSP government even though the PSP had won only 19 seats in a House of 117.

The offer was accepted, and local PSP chief Pattam Thanu Pillai put a ministry together. (It was the kind of arrangement that Lohia had warned against.) The price for such opportunism was paid within months. Police fired on a crowd demanding a linguistic state and, on hearing the news, Lohia dashed off a telegram in his capacity as general secretary asking the government to resign. One of the main charges that the PSP had made against Congress governments was that they resorted to police firing on the slightest pretext. This precipitated a crisis because

Pattam refused to resign, while the national executive felt that Lohia should have consulted it before firing off the telegram. After mediatory efforts failed, Lohia was expelled and led his followers out of the PSP to form a new Socialist Party.

JP was becoming increasingly disenchanted with party politics at this time and was moving towards bhoodan. In 1954 he refused to accept any elective or other office in the party. But he continued to be concerned about the socialists and in 1957 made an attempt to reunite the party. This led to long talks and exchanges of letters but was fruitless. Lohia's terms for a settlement virtually amounted to a surrender by the PSP and could not be accepted. The socialists have been split ever since. In the same year, 1957, JP gave up even his basic membership of the PSP.

CHAPTER TEN

THE BHOODAN YEARS

IN THE early fifties, JP was subject to two contrary influences. One, his link with the Socialist Party was becoming weaker as a result of the petty squabbles among the leadership and his disenchantment with political parties in general as agents of change and progress. The second was the magnetism of Vinoba Bhave's bhoodan campaign. Step by step he severed his ties with the party and threw himself into bhoodan, not merely as a method of peaceful land redistribution but also to lay the foundations of a partyless form of democracy in which decisions were taken by consensus on the model of the village panchayat.

But he realized that this was a distant goal that could be achieved only after class and caste distinctions had disappeared through a process of mass political education. It was education and awareness rather than political power or legislation that could bring about this total revolution. But what should people do until this change took place? His reply, contained in a letter to the national executive of the PSP after he had withdrawn from party office, was most significant in view of misinformed or hostile criticism later:

"Even though I believe in, and am working for, a non-party democracy," he said, "I would like to see parliamentary democracy with which India is officially experimenting, to work as successfully as possible. I fear that a failure of this experiment may not prepare the ground so much for my concept of democracy, but for one-party government, which would be a tragedy for India and perhaps also for Asia. I therefore do not find any inconsistency in working for a non-party democracy and at the same time wishing the success of parliamentary democracy... (there is) no reason, without creating a better alternative system,

The Bhoodan Years

to let the present experiment fail." He did not stop writing articles and theses. It was in this period in fact, that he wrote his best pieces explaining his shift from socialism to sarvodaya.

With a new republican constitution in force which provided for adult suffrage, the main task before the country, as JP saw it, was mass education in how best to use the vote. Gandhi had suggested the transformation of the Congress into a Lok Sewak Dal for this purpose, but his advice was rejected by Nehru, Patel, and others who wanted to ride to power on the crest of popularity gained by the Congress for securing independence. For them mass political awareness would be a hindrance because they viewed the state as the only originator and instrument of change. Only a small group of Sarvodaya Samaj and Sarva Sewa Sangh workers, headed by Vinoba Bhave, were trying to follow Gandhi's teachings.

This was the time that the communists had decided to establish a foothold in Telengana, a wild rocky area ideal for guerrilla operations. It was openly described as India's Yenan, the remote province in which Mao had established his rule before taking over the rest of China. Social disparities were very wide in Telengana, with a few persons owning most of the arable land. Even so, the communist guerrillas were not doing too well because India's road and rail communications were better than China's and it was easier to rush police and troops to the area. The guerrillas had the sympathy of the landless labour, but not too many approved of the communist tactics of murder, arson and looting. It was in this area that Vinoba embarked on a walking tour to carry the message of non-violence. He turned down the government offer of an armed escort and walked from village to village accompanied only by five or six workers.

There was little response until in one village an old landless worker pointed towards the big landowners clustered around Vinoba. They owned thousands of acres, he said, but did no work. It was poor labourers like himself who produced the grain that made the landlords affluent, but got barely enough to subsist on themselves. What good could Vinoba's teaching of ahimsa do in these circumstances? Vinoba had no ready answer. He asked the landless how much land they would require. They conferred together, said 80 acres. He wondered aloud how this land could be obtained and made the point that no one could really claim complete ownership of land, because it was not provided by God to them. At the most, they could be regarded as trustees given the responsibility of making the best use of it. After some minutes, an elderly patriarch stood up from among the landowners and offered to donate a 100 acres to the landless. The date was 18 April 1951 and the name of the village, Pochampalli. That was the start of the bhoodan movement.

JP became interested in the bhoodan approach soon after. He had been searching for an effective non-violent instrument for social change, but found it neither in Marxism nor parliamentary democracy. So he took readily to the thesis that land reform and village democracy could be set up by persuasion and conciliation. That appeared to be the only solution. He called on Vinoba at the Paunar ashram in August and went round the institutions that had taken root around Gandhi's ashram at Wardha. He was so impressed with the constructive work being done that he remarked that he had found "a group of bold and original entrepreneurs who are in far greater touch with the people and their problems than any other group in the country."

At the Pachmarhi conference of the Socialist Party he had already interpreted the party's bad showing in Gandhian terms. "We failed because we had not put in enough work. Work is not merely waging the class struggle. There is constructive work which we have sadly neglected... We must try to understand Acharya Vinoba Bhave's efforts and not ridicule them. It is another matter whether his efforts can solve the land problem or not. One thing is certain, he is focusing the attention of the people and the government on this problem....Vinoba Bhave is a spark of the revolutionary force of Gandhism. If this spark and the Socialist Party combine, it can shake up the whole country and start a big conflagration against injustice." This suggestion was incorporated in a resolution and unanimously adopted by the party. And to demonstrate his own commitment to bhoodan, JP donated half of his 50 acres of land to the movement.

Three weeks before his fast in June, he met Vinoba again at Banda and was with him for three hours. After recovering from the fast, he spent more and more time on bhoodan work, especially in Gaya district. In one week he collected pledges for 7,000 acres. He was greatly moved by this experience because he found that the poorer landowners were far more willing to donate land than the richer ones. He felt a sense of kinship with them and the experience was as much of a landmark in his life as listening to Abul Kalam Azad's speech in his student days in Patna, his conversion to Marxism in the United States, and the talks in Nasik jail that led to the formation of the Congress Socialist Party.

From now on he referred to the bhoodan movement with all the zeal of a new convert. He spoke of it at the first Asian Socialist Conference in Rangoon, and in his letter to Nehru containing the 14 points. ("I do not find today Gandhiji's dynamism and incessant quest towards his ultimate values except in Vinoba who has produced a remarkable Gandhian method for the solution of the country's biggest problem—the land problem.") He came back to the subject at the Betul conference where he explained that bhoodan was not asking for charity, but a demand for realization of rights. It was "an experiment in non-violent economic revolution." And to place Vinoba's achievement in perspective, he pointed out that before he toured the area, "two and a half years of communist violence had resulted in over 3,000 murders and the destruction of property worth more than six crores." And also that more land had been distributed to the landless through bhoodan than through all the land reform laws passed by the legislature.

The feeling that he was actually changing the pattern of life in some areas gave him far more satisfaction than the unending squabbles over ideology, policy and status in which political parties were involved. At the sarvodaya conference at Chandil in 1953, he tried hard to involve young people in sarvodaya work. He got an immediate response, with students from as far as Calcutta dedicating themselves to the bhoodan movement. This was the first occasion that he tried to draw students into the struggle, an appeal he would make again on a far vaster scale.

JP's clear thinking at the time (1953) was reflected in an article in *Janata* titled "A Plea for Gandhism." In it he said: "Gandhism does not concentrate on the capture of power of the state, but goes direct to the people and helps them to effect the revolution in their lives and, consequently, revolution in the life of the community... the Gandhian technique necessarily goes beyond the confines of party and class, because it aims at converting or revolutionising members of all parties and classes. Socialism wishes to advance by setting class against class; Gandhism by cutting across classes. Socialism wishes to destroy classes by making one class victorious over the other—which seems to be somewhat illogical. Gandhism wishes to abolish classes by so bringing the classes together that there are no class distinctions left." Both socialism and Gandhism aimed at a stateless society, but unlike socialism, Gandhism wanted to begin the process here and now.

The inevitable occurred in April 1954. At a sarvodaya conference at Bodh Gaya where Lord Buddha found enlightenment, he announced that he had become a *jeevandani*—one who had dedicated his life to bhoodan; nearly 600 young men and women followed his example. Vinoba was very moved. Though he had begun the campaign, he wrote a note to JP which read: "In response to your call of yesterday, here is the offering of my own life for the establishment of a non-violent social order based on bhoodan yagna and with village industries as its mainstay." Prabhavati, who had been a staunch Gandhian all along, was even happier. She thanked God for bringing this day into her life. The only element of sadness was that Gandhi was not there to witness it.

JP's jeevandan made a big impression. For it was known that he would have been second to Nehru in the Union government had he accepted the Prime Minister's offer to join his cabinet. Even without joining the government at this stage, he was popular enough all over the country to be regarded as Nehru's most likely successor. To have given up politics in these circumstances was a major act of renunciation. Explaining his decision in an article in *Janata*, he reminded his leaders that bhoodan "does not aim at capturing the state... it does not wish to create or become a political party... it aims rather at persuading the people, independently of what the state may or may not want, to carry out a revolution in their own lives, and through that a revolution in society.... It aims further at creating those conditions in which the people may manage their affairs directly, without the intermediation of parties and parliaments....The device of democratic elections cannot quite equate five hundred representatives with 18 crores (counting only the adults) of the people. To the extent that the 18 crores look after their affairs directly, to that extent the powers and functions of the State are restricted and real democracy is practised."

JP set up an ashram in Sokhodevra, a remote village on the border between Gaya and Hazaribagh districts, where he had halted for a night during his flight from Hazaribagh Jail twelve years earlier. Here he opened a basic work and rural centre to train village level workers. Within a few years, the area was transformed by creating *bunds* (earth dams) to trap rainwater and use it for irrigation, digging new channels, levelling the ground and introducing unsophisticated rural technology. Prabhavati spent the happiest days of her life there.

But JP could not bury himself in the ashram completely. He felt called upon to issue statements on national and international developments that touched him deeply. He was also anxious to reunite the socialists as the only group that could function as a democratic opposition and alternative to the Congress. But, as noted earlier, he was unable to come to terms with Lohia, and the correspondence between them lost all traces of the camaraderie that was evident before. This split was one of the biggest reasons for the decline of the socialist movement in India.

On 12 August 1975, for instance, JP actually wrote out a letter to Lohia and handed it to him to minimize the possibility of misunderstanding. In such circumstances, the language could only be cold and formal. But the rank and file of the party and sympathizers outside could not appreciate the factors keeping JP and Lohia apart and pushing JP towards bhoodan.

At the second conference of the PSP at Gaya in 1955, slogans were shouted to the effect that socialism was coming and JP would bring it. But he told them quite frankly that he had no magic wand to bring in socialism. He now saw the bhoodan approach as the only way out of the country's problems. In fact he had only stayed on in the party until the 1957 general elections because it had been badly hit by the secession of the Lohia group and the death of the veteran and respected Marxist theoretician, Acharya Narendra Deva. He now resigned even his ordinary membership of the party and distributed a letter to members explaining the decision.

For two decades after his call on Vinoba in 1951, JP devoted himself to bhoodan not only as a method of land redistribution but also as a means to promote village self-government (gramswarajya) as the structure on which a real democracy would be based. The campaign went fairly well in the fifties. Pledges for nearly a million acres had been collected by the end of the

The Bhoodan Years

decade and though the pace slowed thereafter, Vinoba Bhave could claim that about 90 per cent of the inhabited area of Bihar had committed itself to gramdan. This meant that at least 75 per cent of the residents of the village, owning at least 51 per cent of the land, had signed the gramdan pledge.

In the early years the provisions were fairly strict. Those who took the pledge renounced private ownership of the land and handed the title over to the village community. But in fact possession and ownership rights were retained except that the owner promised not to sell, mortgage or otherwise part with land to anyone outside the village. Vinoba began by asking landowners to give one-sixth of their land to the landless, but when the response began to fall, reduced the requirement to one-twentieth. JP was reportedly most unhappy with this modification but accepted Vinoba's decision. There was no alternative since Vinoba firmly opposed anything approaching coercion to get results, even the kind of peaceful satyagraha that Gandhi sanctioned in such circumstances. Landowners were also required to contribute one seer out of every maund (one-fortieth) of their produce to the *gram kosh* (village fund). Similarly wage-earners were expected to contribute one day's salary to the gram kosh, and landless workers, one day's free labour to a village project.

Every adult resident in the village was a member of the gram sabha which managed village affairs. Its decisions were taken unanimously or by an overwhelming consensus—say 90 per cent. This was intended to minimize that spirit of factionalism encouraged by the majority principle. In effect this meant that the decisions would have to be acceptable to all the major castes and other groups inhabiting a village. Ideally, representatives to district, state, and even national legislatures could also be selected by consensus, thus avoiding the disruptive impact of party politics. To see that the traditionally higher castes did not dominate, the sabha became one of the primary educational functions of sarvodaya and other than non-political social service workers.

There would have been enough workers if Gandhi's advice to convert the Congress into a Lok Sewak Sangh had been accepted. In any case the very act of Brahman and Harijan sitting at the same meeting gradually eroded caste barriers. It was process, a change of values, that was beginning, not an instant revolution.

Up to 1957, the government did not do much to help or hinder the bhoodan movement. But that year the Sarva Sewa Sangh organized a conference of political leaders to coordinate strategy at Yelwal (Mysore). Among those who attended were Nehru, Govind Ballabh Pant, Gulzarilal Nanda, Morarji Desai and Namboodiripad. They decided to keep community developments free of politics and that the Sarva Sewa Sangh and the community projects administration would try to coordinate their work. By 1959, panchayati raj institutions (panchayats are executive committees of gram sabhas) were created in Rajasthan and other states.

But the system did not work because the panchayats did not enjoy enough autonomy and were subject to governmental pressures. JP's advice was that all public lands be vested with the gram panchayats and that they should exercise real authority over the civil servants under their charge. This, of course, was unacceptable to a cadre of civil servants who had no real faith in democracy, or to the ministers who distributed patronage through them. Nor did political parties refrain from interfering in municipal and panchayat affairs. The official excuse for retaining power over the panchayats was that they might abuse it. While admitting the possibility, JP pointed out that there was no assurance against abuse at higher levels. And this was becoming frequent. At the village level, the culprit could be discovered easily, but not at the higher levels of administration.

These problems had yet to emerge when JP went on a tour of Europe, full of confidence in the bhoodan movement. He visited similar institutions, among them Lanza del Vasto's ashram in the south of France, Daleno Dolci in Sicily and other Gandhians throughout Europe. He was particularly impressed by the amount of voluntary work done in Europe without waiting for or expecting government help.

On his return from Europe, JP was invited to address members of parliament on 23 September 1958. It was right there, in the domed central hall of parliament, that he suggested to the assembled MPs that the system they represented "is not suited to our country; this democratic system which we are running is a game of a very small class of people....I do not think that merely because there is an opposition party or there are opposition parties, there is a guarantee of democracy. The real guarantee of democracy is the faith of the people in democracy, the strength of the people, the capacity of the people to run democracy, the capacity of the people to manage their affairs themselves.

"This is not happening in our country. And, as we are going today, I do not think this is going to happen in the future either; and this is a great danger. Out of this anything may emerge, even a dictatorship of the left or the right, one does not know." And, stressing a point that would become crucial later: "Just because the people participate once in five years or a given number of years in the election of their representatives, you cannot say there is democracy."

Then talking about his concept of partyless democracy that had emerged from bhoodan, JP said quite categorically: "I personally believe and fully believe that it is possible to develop a partyless democracy. But I am not asking you here and now to abolish the party system. Nobody would be prepared for it and it would be foolish to do that today because there is nothing to take its place." He made two suggestions for a beginning. One was not particularly new—that parties keep away from local body elections. But he was not willing to leave this to the parties—they had broken such agreements before. He proposed a law that would prohibit any candidate from using the name of a party or flying its flag, and disallow any party from supporting a particular candidate.

The second suggestion was new and more important in the light of future developments. This concerned the selection of candidates. They were usually nominated by the election boards of the various parties and all the voters could do was to choose between them. Instead, he suggested a procedure similar to the American primaries and the system he found being practised in Yugoslavia. This was that all the voters of a particular polling booth get together and select two delegates. Together with other delegates from other booths in the same constituency, they elect a number of candidates. For instance, anyone who receives more than a certain minimum number of votes (say 25 per cent of the total) is eligible to stand for election to the legislature. It is only at this stage that political parties adopt a candidate. Until then they are expected to confine their activities to educating the electorate about their policies and programmes without backing any specific candidates.

But with Nehru still alive and the ruling elite equating democracy with the type practised at Westminster, these suggestions received little support. As JP put it himself, sarvodaya was regarded as a crankish, old-fashioned creed. The time for it to be given serious consideration was yet to come because the failure of the various Western (including Soviet) development models had not become obvious. But the disabilities of over-centralization had begun to show. At the local self-government conference in Bangalore in November 1960, JP could not help commenting sarcastically: "I have often felt that Delhi is the burial place of Mahatma Gandhi in more senses than one."

By this time, the bhoodan campaign had lost its early appeal. Some of the donated land was found to be of poor quality, some plots were too small for a living, there were legal hurdles to transfer of property and some of the donors had second thoughts and took back their land forcibly. Also there were just not

The Bhoodan Years

enough workers to achieve the huge target set for them—50 million acres. The organizers had neglected the towns from which many selfless student workers could have been drawn (as JP did later). It was only in 1957 that Vinoba thought of recruiting the *Tarun Shanti Sena* (youth brigade) to carry the bhoodan message deep into the countryside, but by then the momentum of the movement was declining.

Though Vinoba and JP agreed on essentials, they operated on a different time scale. Vinoba was not particularly concerned with how long a process took; he wanted to instil the right moral ideas and hoped that in time people would be converted to it in large enough numbers to create a social revolution by consent. He had no use for coercion, even of the gentle Gandhian variety, because in that case it would not be a genuine conversion. Neither Gandhi nor JP had so much patience. They did not want the process of change to take any longer than necessary because delay meant so much more suffering for so many. They drew the line at violence only because it had its own evil repercussions.

This difference in approach came to the surface in relation to the Bihar movement. The entire Sarva Sewa Sangh almost broke on this issue at a conference in Wardha in July 1974. Out of the 24 members in the working committee, 21 sided with JP in wanting the Sangh to be fully involved in the movement. But three were opposed and the Sangh convention was that all decisions must be taken unanimously. After a long discussion with Vinoba, he agreed to a formula that allowed each worker to follow the dictates of his own conscience. But his disapproval was evident in the way he put it: "I would agree with whatever JP chooses to do on his own because I know (a) that JP is a gentleman, (b) that he would decide to do only that which will lead to the good and he would do it with no personal axe to grind, (c) that he would certainly own his mistake if he later realised it and would correct it, and (d) lastly that nothing is going to come out of this agitation." But the unanimity was superficial. The majority of the workers followed JP into Bihar and gave the movement an unselfish non-partisan character it would not have had otherwise; but a handful continued to work against him.

CHAPTER ELEVEN

ALTERNATIVES TO VIOLENCE

ALTHOUGH INVOLVED in the bhoodan campaign, JP did not cut himself off from events in the country and abroad. He reacted promptly to issues involving violence and suppression. When he heard about the Soviet attack on Hungary in 1956 and the failure of India's representative at the United Nations to condemn it, he said: "As an Indian I hang my head in shame that a spokesman of my country (Krishna Menon) should have gone so far in cynical disregard of the truth and the fundamental principles of freedom and peace." In March 1959 came the Chinese occupation of Tibet. "We cannot physically prevent the Chinese from annexing Tibet," he said, "but we are not serving the cause of peace by slurring over aggression." He went on to organize an international conference on Tibet in Delhi. The Dalai Lama, who had managed to escape to India, wrote thanking him for championing Tibet's cause.

As a man of principle, he did not take up only popular issues. He criticized the Government of India for marching troops into Goa in 1961. Though anxious to have Goa united with the rest of the country, he felt there was no excuse for resorting to violence. He justified violent resistance when China marched its forces across the Himalayas towards Assam and Ladakh in 1962 but was always anxious for a peaceful settlement. In 1963, he organized a "friendship march" from New Delhi to Peking with Shankarrao Deo and some foreign pacifists but was denied passage through Pakistan and entry into China. He set up an India-Pakistan conciliation group in 1962 and two years later visited Pakistan in an attempt to create links between influential persons on both sides. He was quite optimistic after meeting President Ayub, but the outbreak of war between the countries in 1965 ended that initiative. Some of the parties following him now called him a traitor at that time.

Yet another peace mission took him to Nagaland, on India's border with Burma. The tribal area had been in a state of insurgency ever since the Government of India had tried to extend its administration into the area which had gained strategic importance owing to the proximity of Chinese territory. Many of the Nagas resisted and the Indian army had to be called in to maintain some semblance of order. JP took a peace mission into the area in 1964 and the team managed to bring about a truce. As the only individuals trusted by both sides, they were able to head off several confrontations. But JP resigned from the peace mission in February 1965 because a statement by him was interpreted by some Naga leaders as being biased in favour of New Delhi. His colleagues stayed on. An extract from one of his speeches on the Naga problem shows the combination of nationalist and liberal that has always marked his views on issues with foreign involvements. However much he may differ from New Delhi's handling of the issue, he has never conceded the right of interference to any foreign government even if, as in the case of Pakistan, he was also involved in trying to improve relations with it.

Writing on the Nagn issue, JP blamed a misunderstanding by some Nagas, of the implications of being part of the Indian Union, and the inept handling of the issue by the Union and Assam governments, for friction. The point he made was that the Nagas had lived for more than half a century under British rule and when India became free, the Nagas became part of the free and democratic Indian community. But they failed to appreciate the change and treated their relations with the rest of India on the same basis as they had treated their relations with Britain, which was a colonial one. "Under British rule," he explained, "the Nagas were a subject people; now they are a part, like the Assamese for instance, of the free and democratic people of India. Nagaland is not a colony or dependency of India, ruled and exploited by India, but just like any other Indian state, it is self-governing with its proportionate (or even more than proportionate) share in the affairs of the Indian government."

Had the Indian administrators taken the same view and not behaved as if they were the successors of the British, the problem could have been resolved long ago, with Nagaland given maximum autonomy under the Indian Union.

JP's approach to the Kashmir issue was similar. He recognized the justice of much of Sheikh Abdullah's case though this made him unpopular with communal Hindu opinion. He wrote to Mrs Gandhi in June 1966, soon after she became Prime Minister, urging the release of Sheikh Abdullah as the only way to work out a settlement. He was brutally frank: "We profess secularism but let Hindu nationalism stampede us into trying to establish it by repression. Kashmir has distorted India's image for the world as nothing else has done. . . ."

But he was no less frank in addressing a convention in Srinagar in 1968 where the Sheikh was present. He described the interest of international forces in the strategic area and ruled out the possibility of an independent Kashmir. Then he went on to add: "These are unpleasant but inescapable realities, and as your friend and well-wisher I am bound to speak the truth as I see it. This convention must understand clearly that after the 1965 conflict (with Pakistan) no Government of India can accept a solution which placed Kashmir outside the Union of India. Or to put it positively, a solution has to be found within the framework of India." Several Kashmiri leaders did not take too kindly to this advice at the time, but years later, the kind of settlement proposed by JP was at last being given a chance.

Even before independence, communal discord was a constant source of anxiety to JP. He was one of the few who, with Gandhi, did not celebrate 15 August 1947 as independence day.

For them it meant partition of the country and therefore not the complete independence they had struggled for. Transfer of power, the British description of the event, seemed more appropriate.

Well before the transfer, in his writings while confined in Lahore fort, JP had opposed any negotiations with the Muslim League, and predicted that partition would be no solution because the root cause of communal tension was economic and political rather than religious. Since then, he has done his best to pacify and inquire into such major communal outbreaks as at Jabalpur, Ranchi and Ahmedabad. While usually finding Hindus, the majority community, at fault, he did not hesitate to blame Muslim communalism when necessary.

His presidential address to the second national convention against communalism in December 1968 spared nobody. He found that parties that professed their faith in secularism had done nothing to educate the public about it. In fact some of them, by adopting a policy of accommodation towards the communal minded parties just for a share in political power, have helped spread communalism among the people.

"India being a country of many religions, almost every religious community has its own brand of communalism. They are all pernicious, but Hindu communalism is more pernicious than the others. One reason is that because Hindus constitute a great majority of the population of India, Hindu communalism can easily masquerade as Indian nationalism and denounce all opposition to it as anti-national. Some like the Rashtriya Swayamsevak Sangh (RSS) might do it openly by identifying the Indian nation with Hindu Rashtra; others might do it more subtly."

Even though JP had drifted some distance away from Nehru, they had the same approach to secularism and he was profoundly moved on hearing of his death on 27 May 1964. He said that the ship of state had lost its captain. Another personal loss was the death of Lohia in October 1967. After a long period of estrangement, they had begun to come closer. JP admitted much later that he had found that Lohia was right in some of the issues on which they had differed, like his emphasis on struggle.

In August 1965, JP travelled to Manila to receive the Magsaysay award for outstanding public service from the President of the Philippines. The amount was invested and fetched Rs 400 in interest per month, which was enough to meet his personal everyday expenses. Friends helped him out when he was travelling on a mission of national importance.

Although he possibly would not accept the fact himself, he began losing faith in persuasion as a technique of building up gramdan towards the end of the sixties. The realization that a measure of moral pressure was also required came with the new decade. On 31 May 1970, when he was at Pauri in Uttarakhand, he got a letter telling him that two respected Gandhian workers, Badri Narain Sinha and Gopalji Mishra, president and secretary of the Muzaffarpur district sarvodaya mandal, had been served with death notices by Naxalites. The execution dates mentioned were 5 and 7 June. He and his wife immediately left for the area, which is in the neglected part of Bihar, north of the Ganga, and announced on arrival at Muzaffarpur that they proposed to stay in the Musahari development block of the district.

The threats proved to be empty although Naxalites had been accused of four murders committed in the area. JP's reaction was not only of anxiety, but also a kind of elation. He had been feeling for some time that the gramdan movement and the sarvodaya workers involved in it had grown stale. As he put it himself later: "The emergence of such danger to our lives appeared to me a godsend. I had been feeling for quite some time past that our movement was losing its fire, and we, its workers, were becoming stale and flabby of spirit. One of the reasons for this seemed to be that our work was so bland that it involved no personal danger to us, nor demanded any great sacrifice."

His continued stay in one small area of a district, moving every few days from one impoverished village to another, listening to complaints and experiences, made him realize how little independence, and the plans made since then, had affected such areas. It also gave him an insight into the inadequacies of the sarvodaya effort which would lead to a decision that would mark another important milestone in his life.

JP issued a statement on his arrival in the area that in his view Naxalism was "primarily a social, economic, political and administrative problem" and "only secondarily a law and order question." He was concerned only with the primary aspect. And he found enough reasons for rural frustration to explode into violence, though he repeatedly made the point that violence could not be a remedy.

For instance, he found that for several reasons legal redress was simply not available to the really poor and exploited. In a pamphlet on his experiences in Musahari, he wrote: "My first reaction on coming face to face with this reality was to realise how remote and unreal were the brave pronouncements of Delhi or Patna from the actuality of the ground level. High-sounding words, grandiose plans, reforms galore. But somehow they all, or most of them remained suspended somewhere in midair."

The reasons he gave for the increase in politically-motivated violence in rural areas amounted to a formidable indictment of society and government: "It is not the so-called Naxalites who have fathered this violence, but those who have persistently defied and defeated the reform laws for the past so many years—be they politicians, administrators, landowners or money-lenders. The big farmers who cheated the ceiling law through *benami* and fictitious settlement; the gentlemen who grabbed government lands and village commons; the landowners who persistently denied the legal rights of their share-croppers and evicted them from their holdings or underpaid their labourers and threw them out from their homestead; the men who by fraud or force took the lands from the weaker sections; the so-called upper-caste men who looked down upon their harijan brethren; the money-lenders who charged usurious interest rates and seized the lands of the poor and the weak; the politicians, the administrators and all the others who aided and abetted these wrongs—it is they who are responsible for the accumulated sense of injustice, grievance and hurt among the poor down-trodden that is now seeking its outlet in violence.

"Also responsible are the courts of law where the procedures and costs of justice have conspired to deny a fair deal to the weaker sections of our society. Responsible again is the system of education and the kind of planning that is producing an ever-expanding army of ill-educated, frustrated and unemployed youth, and which accentuates economic disparities and leads to further polarization of classes. Responsible yet again are the politicians, whose self-seeking has reduced democracy, the party system, and the ideologies to a farce."

But JP took equal pains to explain that violence was no remedy. First of all, he pointed out that violence did not necessarily lead to social revolution. It could produce a reaction and end up in a fascist dictatorship. Or it could end up in chaos, mass misery and disintegration and enslavement of the nation. Second, social and historical conditions had to be ripe for a revolution to succeed. They did not happen at the will of revolutionaries. Third, he drew attention to the negative aspects of invoking violence. The old order was destroyed, but history had shown that thereafter the revolutionaries entered into a fratricidal bloodbath among themselves and in fact not a single revolution had realized the ideals for which it was begun. Lenin's slogan "all power to the soviets" had not come about more than fifty years after the Russian revolution and "there still happens to be a party dictatorship clamped down upon the Russian people." The fourth negative consequence of a violent revolution was that "power comes invariably to be usurped by a handful of the most ruthless among the erstwhile revolutionaries." This was inevitable "when power comes out of the barrel of a gun and the gun is not in the hands of the common people....That is why a violent revolution has always brought forth a dictatorship of some kind or the other. And that is also why after a revolution a new privileged class of rulers and exploiters grows up in the course of time to which the people at large are once again subject."

This brought JP to the crucial question of what should be done in such circumstances. He went back to Gandhi for an answer. "While the rest of the national leaders relied solely on the power of the state to accomplish their task of nation-building, Gandhiji was clear in his mind that the State could never be the sole instrument for creating the India of his dreams.... He did not underestimate the role of the State, nor was he uninterested in its proper and effective working....Nevertheless he clearly saw that even with the best of policies and the best of men in command, the State by itself could not deliver the goods." JP's solution was modelled on Gandhi's teaching which was "to create the power of the people alongside the power of the State. Accordingly, he was preparing to go back to the people at the head of a large band of revolutionary workers, to serve the people, to educate and change them, and set them up on their feet, to involve them directly in the process of social change and reconstruction. His means were going to be, as before, service, constructive work and 'conversion by gentle persuasion, and when the situation required, non-violent non-cooperation or resistance'."

JP was not too happy with the progress of the gramdan movement. He praised Vinoba for collecting constructive workers in the Sarva Sewa Sangh and sending them out with a programme of "conversion by gentle persuasion." Although some progress had been made in redistributing land, the pace was slow: "So far we have not come across a single village where we have found the two requirements of 75 per cent of the population owning 51 per cent of the land to have been fulfilled."

Among the reasons he gave was the decay of personal morality to the extent that even those who had signed the bhoodan pledges were trying to wriggle out of the commitment. But he obviously did not want to sound too pessimistic and so commented rather lamely: "Yet our short experience shows, as noted earlier, that consistent friendliness and manifest concern for everybody's good, coupled with patient persuasion and education, do ultimately succeed." One other sign of progress that he noted was that gramdan and sarvodaya had replaced Naxalism and Naxalite exploits as the main topic of conversation in the villages.

JP criticized the Naxalites on two counts. One was that their methods were terroristic rather than revolutionary and he was proved right in anticipating that "terroristic violence, in fact, is more likely to provoke counter-violence from the stronger sections of society, leading eventually to some form of despotism." The second was the anti-nationalism implied in such slogans as "Chairman Mao is our Chairman too." In spite of these faults, he found that "the very impatience of the Naxalites with the existing state of affairs had an appealing quality. Moreover, their attempt to precipitate a revolution here and now has rendered at least one service, in that it has aroused the social consciousness of the people in general and prodded the powers that be, in particular, to hasten the implementation of the land and other socio-economic reforms."

This indirect praise for the Naxalites shocked some but JP had gone even further in an address to the national conference of voluntary agencies on, of all occasions, the Gandhi Centenary Year. Many of the points he made, especially about the ineffectiveness of violence, were the same as he made at Musahari, but he shocked many of his sarvodaya colleagues by putting the issue far more bluntly. "What India needs today on her political agenda is non-violent social revolution. Not only from the moral point of view, (because) otherwise violence will grow...My sarvodaya friends and my Gandhian friends will be surprised to read what I publicly say now. I say with a due sense of responsibility that if I myself am convinced that there is no deliverance for the people except through violence, then Jayaprakash Narayan will also take to violence. If the problems of the people cannot be solved democratically, I will also take to violence. I am raising these fundamental questions because otherwise observance of the Gandhi Centenary is meaningless. I am not interested in it unless we do something to change the social order."

Late in 1971, JP fell ill. He had been suffering from sciatica and diabetes for some time. Now there were signs of a heart condition. On medical advice, he cut down his engagements and then announced that he would accept no public engagement until his 70th birthday on 11 October 1972. But when he found that he could play a part in persuading the notorious dacoits of the Chambal valley to surrender, he accepted the challenge.

He also became closely involved in the struggle for Bangladesh. Here, again, it was his reputation for independence and integrity that enabled him to clear up some of the inevitable differences that arose between the Awami League leaders and Indian officials. He was on such good terms with acting Bangladesh Premier Tajuddin Ahmed that he sent him a letter advising the new Bangladesh Government not to follow the Indian model of centralized planning and wide wage differential. Unfortunately, the advice was not taken.

JP went round the principal capitals of the world in 1971 to explain India's and Bangladesh's case. Since it was widely known that he was no official propagandist and did not hesitate to differ with his government, his views were heard with great respect

Alternatives to Violence

and played a major part in persuading people, if not their governments, of the justice of Bangladesh's case and its urgent need for international assistance.

A second venture involved journeying in the notorious ravines of the Chambal river which dacoits had used as a base for generations. Armed police and paramilitary units had been unable to flush the dacoits from their hiding place for decades. In 1960 a small group had surrendered to Vinoba Bhave, but there was no follow-up. After a lapse of 11 years, Madho Singh, one of the most notorious dacoits, with a price of Rs 150,000 on his head, approached JP and identified himself. He wanted JP to arrange for a surrender in which the dacoits would not lose face and would not have to face the death sentence. Although preoccupied with the problems of Bangladesh, JP agreed to contact the state governments of Madhya Pradesh, Rajasthan and Uttar Pradesh, the areas in which the dacoits had operated.

The governments responded favourably and JP went into the heart of the dacoit country without any guards to negotiate the surrender. The unarmed Gandhian workers accompanying him got to know the dacoits very well—so much so that some police officials complained that the dacoits, who had committed many murders and other crimes, were being lionized. But JP had succeeded in doing what the government could not—persuade the outlaws not only to surrender their arms but also repent their crimes. In a touching gesture, the notorious Mohar Singh bowed before Prabhavati and touched her feet, while she placed the auspicious vermilion *tilak* on his forehead.

Even more dramatic was Mohar Singh's surrender before the police. He carried his trusted rifle towards a statue of Gandhi, raised it above his head and then went down on his knees to place it at the foot of the statue. He did the same with his ammunition belt. More than 400 wanted dacoits followed his example in the next few days. A declaration was read out on their behalf. It said: "We the inhabitants of the Chambal valley, whose activities until now have brought much suffering to all the people, today surrender ourselves for the service of society from now onwards. We are starting an altogether new life with the blessings of Baba Vinoba and Babu Jayaprakash Narayan.

"We have committed many mistakes and misdeeds for which our hearts are full of genuine remorse. We ask forgiveness from all those who had to suffer some loss or the other on our account. Our only prayer to God Almighty is may He grant us the moral strentgh to walk on the path of righteousness and may He make us worthy members of this society in this life itself."

Nothing could have illustrated more graphically the teaching of Gandhi, Vinoba and JP—that moral persuasion and conciliation can have far more resulting effects than force. At the same time it was equally true that the dacoits would not have considered surrender if the police were not making their lives uncomfortable. A combination of both persuasion and pressure was obviously required, but this was not recognized by Vinoba.

CHAPTER TWELVE

BACK TO STRUGGLE

JP is not the kind of political theoretician who is unmoved by actual human suffering and expresses worry about the masses only at a comfortable distance. Time after time he organized relief missions to provide some sustenance to the millions of Biharis who were victims of flood and drought. The operation he mounted during the unprecedented drought in 1966-67 saved half a million lives according to foreign observers. This was because his reputation for integrity attracted volunteers and donations from all over the world. It is these activities, even more than his political tours, that have made his name known to every household in Bihar.

Nor is JP the kind of theorist who does nothing because the ultimate goal is distant and unlikely to be achieved in his lifetime, and the improvements that can be made earlier are relatively trivial. He has been following a dual strategy. One is aimed at securing maximum decentralization of power and building up grassroots organizations that can utilize the power for their own development, independent of party pressures. This is an attempt to raise the structure of partyless democracy from the base up. The other is to retain the maximum liberty and freedom available in the Constitution and the parliamentary process so that authoritarianism or chaos does not overtake the country while the decentralized gramraj structure develops.

This has involved countless speeches, articles, seminars and meetings. By itself each one seems to have had no impact. But taken together they have created a climate in which the people have begun to demand change. The evidence can be seen from the reactions of those in power. After taking no notice of obvious weaknesses in the electoral system for 25 years, especially in relation to the expenditure of vast sums of money, the Congress government has begun to talk about methods to end such malpractices (of which it was the principal beneficiary). In December 1973 he wrote to each member of parliament suggesting ways and means to protect the citizens' fundamental rights as laid down in the Constitution (except to property), the independence of the judiciary, and the reduction of administrative and political corruption. For some months before drafting this letter, he had been relatively inactive due to ill-health; and the death of Prabhavati on 15 April that year was a crippling blow. She had been ill with cancer for months, but did not reveal it to him until the last stages because she feared it would impose an added strain on his heart at a time that his doctors had recommended minimum strain. In spite of his bereavement, he visited Bombay to promote the Gandhian ideal of trusteeship in industry, but was obviously tired and exhausted to the extent that many of his friends feared he would not survive his wife too long.

But he pulled himself together by the end of the year. The main reason appears to have been his concern for the direction in which the country was going. The MPs he had written to and party leaders he had met seemed engrossed only in getting whatever they could out of the system. So on 9 December he wrote an open letter to the only force he could think of which would be patriotic and idealistic but also difficult to control—the power of frustrated youth. He appealed to them to launch a Youth for Democracy movement to protect the system. In his letter, he said that "the most serious danger comes from vitiation of the democratic process. The seminal role of elections in the democratic process, and their significance for the people can hardly be overemphasized. But since independence, elections have been growing more and more irrelevant to the people and to the democratic process.

"The reason is that money, falsehood, corruption and physical force have combined to erode steadily the very meaning and substance of elections. Election costs have been growing by leaps and bounds, and cases have been reported in which a single state assembly candidate is said to have spent between Rs 30 to Rs 40 lakhs and a Lok Sabha candidate as much as Rs 60 to Rs 90 lakhs. But even if the cost is one-tenth of these straggering amounts, the poor man's party or candidate has no chance whatever.

"Nor can representatives capable of spending such large sums be ever expected to work for the poor. In the same way, the vice of impersonation, fed on secret funds, and the use of physical force, supported by powerful political and caste interests, have been growing at an alarming rate. Corruption of the electoral machinery, commonly manifested in intimidation and buying up of presiding officers, has been growing apace alongside of corruption in other fields."

After describing this dismal picture, JP asked: "Will our youth continue to look on idly at this strangulation of the democratic process at its very birth? Surely there cannot be a more important issue which should move the youth to action. ... What form their action should take is for the youth themselves to decide. My only recommendation would be that in keeping with the spirit and substance of democracy, it must be scrupulously peaceful and non-partisan."

JP's appeal was answered sooner than expected. In January 1974, a revolt by students over excessive mess bills in hostels at Ahmedabad and Morvi snowballed into a general campaign against the scarcity and rising prices of food and other essential goods. And this in turn widened into a people's movement against corruption in the state government headed by Chimanbhai Patel. Although usually regarded as one of the most disciplined and hardworking people in the country, nothing but the removal of the ministry and dissolution of the assembly could satisfy the Gujaratis. The administration had come to a standstill by the time Prime Minister Indira Gandhi bowed to the popular demand in mid-March. There is no reason to believe that JP's appeal to youth to save democracy had anything to do with the Gujarat uprising. It had not been widely reported in the newspapers. Nor had the student leaders sought his advice. But the coincidence did suggest that JP was right in theorizing that the country was ripe for revolution and any spark would be enough to ignite it. JP visited Gujarat for four days at the invitation of the student leaders, and then went to New Delhi to seek a compromise but fell ill there. The Gujarat students had not formulated any further demand or programme and their movement died down. Even so, the anti-Congress mood was serious enough to prevent Mrs Gandhi from ordering fresh elections even more than a year after the Chimanbhai ministry fell.

The impact of Gujarat on Bihar has already been mentioned. Here the Union government took a totally different line. Though Biharis had much more reason to be dissatisfied with their government, and the movement against it was far more widespread and well-disciplined, the legislature was not dissolved, nor the chief minister changed. This was even after ministers and MLAs were unable to visit their constituencies and the whole of Patna had to be barricaded like a medieval fort to prevent people from demonstrating against a government that was supposed to be popular. Thousands of people, including respected professors and public men, were detained under the same emergency law adopted to enable the government to seize smugglers. But the movement survived, longer than even the longest of Gandhi's movements.

As in Gujarat, the movement was begun by students in Bihar. They had twelve demands, of which eight related to minor university reforms and four reflected the sufferings of the entire population—corruption, high prices, unemployment and the need for fundamental changes in the educational system. A demonstration by the students on 18 March 1974 was countered by indiscriminate police violence. But even worse was the fact that the city was left to gangsters, who significantly, tried to burn down the *Searchlight* offices (a paper that had been critical of the state government and the CPI), and looted many other buildings.

It was only the next day, 19 March, that the students' action committee sought JP's help and guidance. Although still convalescing from illness, he agreed to guide them, on two conditions. One was that they should be peaceful; and second that, even if they belonged to different political parties, they must function unitedly and give the objectives of the movement priority over the programme of their parties. Thus began a unique association between a leader in his seventies and followers in their teens, which would rock the country.

After the Bihar government, presumably under orders from the Centre, had tried to put down the movement as brutally as possible, with unprovoked resort to firing by the police in Patna and Gaya, and wide-ranging arrests of Gandhian workers, a harsher tone entered JP's statements. On 6 April he felt constrained to say: "Those who think that sarvodaya is made up of goody-goody people, who no doubt talk about non-violent revolution but do not mean it seriously, are in for a surprise. Speaking for myself, I cannot remain a silent spectator to misgovernment, corruption and the rest, whether in Patna, Delhi or elsewhere. It is not for this that I at least had fought for freedom.

"I am not interested in this or that ministry being replaced or the assembly being dissolved. These are partisan aims and their achievement will make no difference. It will be like replacing Tweedledum with Tweedledee. But I have decided to fight corruption and misgovernment and blackmarketing, profiteering and hoarding, to fight for the overhaul of the educational system, and for a real people's democracy."

CHAPTER THIRTEEN

THE BIHAR MOVEMENT

As THE Bihar movement spread it began to threaten the system of promoting group and sectarian vote banks and buying them off at election time with the huge sums of black money that the Congress party was able to collect in return for favours. Combined with an electoral system that usually enabled the ruling party to secure a majority of seats with a minority vote owing to the fragmentation of opposition votes, this had ensured Congress control over the Central Government and most state governments. But this comfortable situation was threatend by the exposure of its evils, especially the way in which it had led to the continuing impoverishment of the most backward areas of the country for the benefit of a privileged few. JP had associated demands for electoral reform and an educational system relevant to Indian conditions with the campaign, thus laying bare the entire corrupt network on which Congress party leaders and their rich financiers had fattened.

Mrs Gandhi had not been slow to realise the danger posed by the Bihar movement. Having placed Abdul Gafoor as Chief Minister there, a man who could not survive a day in office without the active support of the Central Government and the central Congrees machine, she was in effect ruling the state by remote control. By 1974 the intelligence and para-military force—steadily expanded since she transferred their control from the Home Ministry to herself—were readily available to carry out her instructions. Technically, the Border Security Force (BSF) had been raised to police the border with China after the cease-fire agreement in 1962 when it was agreed to pull back regular forces. In fact, putting down internal disturbances was an important part of their training. They were far better equipped than the regular police, with some units even trained and equipped to be dropped from the air. More important, they were comprised of men recruited from all over the country who would not feel the inhibitions of the local police at shooting down people who spoke the same language as they.

Many other police intelligence and para-military forces had been raised subsequently, all under New Delhi's control. The latest was the Research and Analysis Wing, soon to become known as RAW, which specialised in CIA-type covert operations which were not, however, limited to foreign countries. The man primarily responsible for organizing these special forces and placing them all under the Prime Minister's charge was her principal secretary, P. N. Haksar, who, fittingly enough, was one of those to be personally humiliated by the machine he had set up, when he fell out of favour for opposing the increasing powers wielded by Sanjay Gandhi.

The powers needed to detain inconvenient citizens had also been acquired and justified by a clever manoeuvre. Soon after the Bihar movement began to hurt, the Central Government initiated a drive against smugglers who had been allowed to profit for years by pandering to the demand for foreign luxury items, like Swiss watches and Scotch whisky, whose import was banned, or for gold which was cheaper abroad than within the country. When some of the leading smugglers were arrested and the volume of smuggling diminished perceptibly, people were most impressed. They overlooked, or justified, the changes made in the Maintenance of Internal Security Act (MISA) that enabled the executive to detain citizens on the flimsiest pretexts because the measure was used mainly against smugglers. The first indications of effective action by the authorities against known criminals were so welcome that the fact that the Government had enough powers under existing laws to do what it had failed to do before went largely unnoticed. Already in Bihar, however, MISA had begun to be used to detain more and more student activists. In time, the same MISA would be deployed to detain the entire opposition leadership and JP himself. This, combined with a country-wide cadre of civil servants, with no local loyalties, and still trained on the colonial model to take orders from the Centre, provided the machinery for authoritarian rule. The fact that westernised academics and intellectuals, including journalists and writers, had a stake in the continuance of an increasingly elitist society also limited protest. The vast majority found one excuse or another to go along with the Government or close their eyes to torture and repression. But few realised, until the declaration of internal emergency on 26 June, 1975, how rotten the elements that were supposed to stand up for democratic rights, had become.

JP, too, shared the widespread delusion that the liberal elements of society and institutions like the press and the judiciary created to counter-balance executive power were strong enough to deter the Government from arresting him and his colleagues. But he did realise how callous and strong the machinery of repression was becoming. He responded by broadening the base of the movement by organising all the militant but peaceful methods of protest devised by Gandhi. At the same time, unlike Gandhi, he made it plain that he expected the movement to be peaceful but not necessarily non-violent. This meant that the demonstrators were not permitted to initiate violence; however, if violence was used against them, he would not call off the campaign if they were provoked into responding violently.

JP's initial reaction to the police brutality and hooliganism in Patna on 18 March 1974, when he agreed to guide the movement started by the Chhatra Sangharsh Samiti (students' action committee) was not militant. In fact, he had a word of praise for the Chief Minister. After making the point that "in any democratic country, after such a monumental failure of administration as Patna witnessed, the Government would have resigned," he went on to say: "From all accounts, Mr Abdul Gafoor is an honourable man with no excessive fondness for office. In that case, my friendly advice to him, in his own and the State's interest, is that he should resign." But Abdul Gafoor was only a pawn in the developing confrontation between JP and the Prime Minister. The decision to deploy maximum force to ensure that the Bihar government should not yield to a student agitation, as had happened in Gujarat two months earlier, had been taken. Three days after the Patna clash, the Government disallowed a silent protest procession organized by the students and arrested several of them. The Bharat Shanti Sena Committee, which was a Sarvodaya organization, was also unable to get permission to take out a silent procession. After this, JP issued a second statement asking the Government to learn to discriminate between organized and planned violence, violence by criminal groups and minor violence like throwing bricks in anger, retaliation or misconceived militancy. He went on to warn, "Unless the pattern of government behaviour changes, I doubt if violence can be curbed." It was in this statement that he said he could not remain a silent spectator to misgovernment.

For a while it seemed as though the government was having second thoughts. JP and several hundred sarvodaya workers and sympathisers were permitted to take out a unique procession on 8 April, in which all the participants tied cotton pieces over their mouths to underline the silent and peaceful nature of their protest. Four days later, however, the police opened fire on demonstrators at Gaya, killing eight. This brought the government's decision to wipe out the movement into the open. After this there was no prospect of retreat by either side. JP had not been keeping too well and on 23 April he left Patna for Vellore for a prostate operation. He was away five weeks, but made sure that the movement did not flag by keeping in daily touch with Acharya Ramamurti, an outstanding sarvodaya worker and former university professor, whom he had nominated to guide it during his absence. He received daily reports and gave his instructions through the teleprinter network of the *Indian Express* group of newspapers, which also published in his weekly *Everyman's*. The movement spread rapidly, with the dissolution of the State Assembly and dismissal of the Gafoor ministry as its main political objectives. In many districts, civil revenue and criminal courts as well administrative offices were virtually closed due to picketing. One of the objectives was to collect ten million signatures demanding dissolution of the assembly, to be presented to the Governor, R.D. Bhandare.

At this point, the Congress, lacking its own cadres, depended on its only ally, the Moscow-oriented Communist Party of India, to pre-empt the campaign. And so, on 3 June, a CPI procession with tribesmen from Chhota Nagpur who knew nothing of the issue, marched through Patna armed with spears, bows and arrows.

A day later, public buses and trains to Patna were cancelled. Trucks carrying students from nearby districts were stopped and seized by the police. BSF units held a flag march through Patna's main streets. Even so, half a million people joined the procession led by JP who presented the ten million signatures to the Governor on 5 June. On the way back, someone opened fire at the procession from a Congress MLA's house. But this did not prevent the crowd, now swollen to more than a million, from filling the Gandhi Maidan to hear JP say more prophetically than he perhaps realised at the time : "Friends, this is total revolution! This is not a movement merely for dissolution of the Bihar Legislative Assembly. We have to go far, very far . . . It will not be easy to act upon the revolutionary ideas that I am going to place before you. You will have to make sacrifice, undergo suffering, face lathis and bullets, fill up jails . . . "

The new elements in the resistance programmes announced by

JP were similar to the civil disobedience movements called by Gandhi during the independence struggle. He asked the people to paralyse the administration at every level, not to pay taxes, close schools (so that students could involve themselves in the campaign and also experiment with new educational techniques and to organize people's power—the grass-roots committees that enabled people to understand their rights and responsibilities, solve their own problems and work towards complete socio-economic change. Part of their function would be to select candidates by consensus to fight in general elections. According to current procedure, the electorate was often asked to vote for candidates completely unknown to the area which left the crucial responsibility of selection to party bosses in the state capital and New Delhi. Thus candidates realised that they owed more to the leader than to those whom they were supposed to represent.

A five week dharna from 7 June on, was organized at the gates of the assembly hall with volunteers from every district in the State present. In all, nearly 30,000 volunteers were arrested in this period. While the movement continued to spread, only twenty members of the Assembly responded to JP's open letter of 18 May, calling upon them to resign because steady deterioration in administration and recourse to "naked violence" had "completely exhausted your mandate"—a comprehensive version of his thesis that constituents should have the right to recall representatives who obviously fail to perform their minimum duties. This limited response was frustrating to the students, but he kept them under control by making the gesture of apologising personally to the speaker when an MLA was manhandled while trying to enter the Assembly building and others were abused. The closure of colleges brought an additional number of recruits into the movement, but it offended many parents. "Are not students and their guardians also aware of the rampant corruption in the state and are they not anxious to have this evil eradicated?" asked JP in an appeal addressed to them. "Are they not, too, being crushed under the weight of rising prices? Are they not also the victims of the wrong policies of the government? Do not these students, too, face the fearful prospect of unemployment?... This is therefore not the time, particularly for young men, to remain idle spectators. They must plunge into the struggle. Examinations are important in a way. But at certain moments of history, there are other things more important than examinations and degrees."

With the Border Security Force, Central Reserve Police and local police unable to repress such a widespread agitation, Congress leaders tried to smear JP personally. This took the familiar form of suggesting that the movement was being financed by the United States. The then Congress president, S.D. Sharma, for instance, said that JP "has been these days working at the instance of hoarders and blackmarketeers... His present campaign appears to me to be part of a pre-planned conspiracy of the right reaction which had its natural allies outside the country." JP's appeal to soldiers and policemen not to obey illegal orders was misrepresented as a call to mutiny and anarchy. This eventually became one of the main excuses for his detention. Mrs Gandhi had started the smear campaign at the Congress meeting at Bhubaneshwar by returning to a charge that she had made before, that "those taking money from the rich have no right to talk about corruption." Repetition had not dulled JP's sensitivity to such charges. He replied once again by drawing attention to an article by him entitled "To My Detractors", first published in *Everyman's* on 12 October, 1973, in which he had given a detailed account of how he maintained himself financially, in response to a similar campaign inspired by the CPI.

The confrontation escalated on both sides. JP's response to mounting repression and the personal attacks on him and his motives was to step up the intensity and widen the range of the movement beyond the borders of Bihar. This was not entirely wise because the movement within the State, which was the primary testing ground of the forces and ideas involved in the confrontation, was apt to lose its edge when he was not there in person to inspire and guide it. It also exposed his inability to mould a set of leaders capable of taking full command in his absence. But as long as he was present in the State that gave the Bihar movement its name, the response to his calls for mass agitation to demonstrate the fact that the people had lost confidence in the State Government and assembly was overwhelming. All activity in Bihar was brought to a complete halt for an unprecedented three days from 3 to 5 October—in response to his call for a state-wide bandh (general strike). The degree of nervousness in the government was reflected in barricades surrounding government buildings and the contingents of armed police and para-military formations—most of them rushed from other states—stationed to guard strategic centres and patrol the main highways and railway tracks. Even so, many trains were immobilised by thousands of people sitting on the tracks. In Patna itself the police opened fire on demonstrators to clear the tracks. To maintain and politicise the emotions aroused by the bandh, JP announced a four-point programme. The first was to extend and intensify the campaign to paralyse administrative work in all government offices at the block and district levels. The second was to utilise popular response to organize the gram-swaraj pattern of administration from the village up to the district level, long attempted by the sarvodaya movement. Linked with this was the third element in the programme, which was to set up a janta sarkar (people's government) if the Central and State governments continued to ignore the demand for the dissolution of the state assembly. The steps to set up a people's assembly in the state would be for each panchayat jana sabha and the Chhatra Sangharsh Samiti in its area to send up five delegates to a constituency council comprised of a hundred delegates (from twenty panchayats). The council would select a legislator from among its members or from outside it. The fourth point was to organize another massive demonstration in Patna on 4 November to express popular support for the dissolution of the assembly. One aspect of the demonstration was to gherao (physically surround) the State secretariat and the houses of ministers and legislators. People were asked to march to Patna from every part of the state to participate in the demonstration. While the attempt to set up a people's administration did not get off the ground, the government's attempt to suppress the mass demonstration had widespread repercussions.

Developments just before the bandh shed some light on Mrs Gandhi's state of mind at the time and, possibly, provided some explanation of what followed. The praise her government received for the round-up of smugglers had not lasted. The arrests had been selective, with many leading smugglers obviously tipped off and others detained in conditions of luxury, with continuing access to the best foreign liquor and female companionship that money could buy. Also, the increasing use of MISA against political opponents was becoming more obvious, with opposition leaders emphasising the threat such powers posed to democracy. No progress was being made in fulfilling the ruling party's election pledges, black money was proliferating, no attempt was being made to execute even those land reforms that had been legislated, and prices were continuing to rise. The next parliamentary elections were due in 16 months, with the mounting tide of public protest touched off by the Bihar movement raising serious doubt about the prospect of Congress securing a working majority. A Congress defeat in a by-election in her home town of Allahabad was seen as a pointer. The fact that the then Chief Minister of Uttar Pradesh, H.N. Bahuguna, was widely believed to have worked against

The Bihar Movement

the Congress candidate, indicated the growing strains within the party. Mrs Gandhi's anxiety to impress public opinion had already been exhibited in the decision to set off an underground nuclear explosion on 18 May. That this was motivated primarily by political rather than scientific or military reasons was clear from the fact that there was no follow-up to the explosion, except in foreign countries.

Ten days before the much-publicised demonstration, JP made a quick tour of Rajasthan and Haryana. The reception he got and the money donated to him for the movement left no doubt about its impact, at least in north India. The last three days were spent in New Delhi, where he announced his future objectives. The primary one was to call a conference of opposition parties, excluding the CPI, to channel "the enthusiasm among the people into a nation-wide people's movement." He was "convinced that total revolution will sweep the country soon and 'yuva shakti' (youth power) will be in the foreground." The aim was not merely to replace the Congress with some other party, but bring about basic changes in the social, economic, political and cultural life of the nation. He also diffused Congress charges that his objective of partyless democracy was unworkable and would, in fact, destroy parliamentary democracy, by reiterating that his concept of partyless democracy could be achieved only in a classless society, which thus seemed to become as remote as the withering away of the state envisaged by Marxism. The fact was, he believed that until local communities gained the ability and confidence to govern themselves through the process of total revolution, parliamentary democracy was the best safeguard against centralised, authoritarian rule.

It was at this stage that Mrs Gandhi invited JP to meet her. They met on 1 November for the first time after the Bihar movement was launched. The formula that was to be the basis of discussion envisaged the resignation of the Gafoor ministry and imposition of President's Rule, suspension of the Bihar assembly until elections were held, release of political prisoners, measures to eradicate corruption and institute educational reforms, and an invitation from the Bihar Governor to JP to end confrontation with the government and work out ways to cooperate with it. JP could continue to guide the people's movement, but in return, should not support the demand for dissolution of other state assemblies. But the talks broke down on the demand for dissolution of the Bihar assembly, which Mrs Gandhi refused to concede and JP refused to give in, in the context of the repressive measures and threatening postures adopted by the state government to put down the proposed bandh.

From the next day, the security arrangements made in Bihar, particularly in Patna, could only be compared to preparations for defending it from a foreign invasion. The tension had been heightened by a brief visit by the new Congress president, Deva Kanta Borooah (who never lived down JP's description of him as court jester), to Patna on 28 October. On the road from the airport into the city, his car ran over and killed a nine-year-old boy. But the nervous official motorcade did not stop and it was left to the police to pick up the body. By 2 November, 60,000 soldiers and policemen were manning key positions in the State, all train and river services to Patna were cancelled, the approaches to the capital were being watched from the air, and about 3,000 people had been arrested. Before the fourth, countless thousands had been detained on the roadside as they trudged towards Patna, but an estimated 50,000 got through.

The demonstration on 4 November soon became a confused spectacle of crowds attempting to approach and follow JP while the BSF and CRP resorted to tear-gassing and numerous lathi charges to disperse them and isolate him from them. JP started out in a jeep but got down to cross barricades and penetrate police cordons. The crucial encounter occurred when a detachment of the Central Reserve Police aimed a volley of tear gas grenades at and around JP and, clearing the crowd with lathi blows, came within striking range of him as he was sitting exhausted on the ground, his eyes streaming and breathing choked from the effects of the tear gas. A group of volunteers formed a human barricade round him, but another group of the burly CRP jawans seemed determined to get at him. Four Bihari plainclothes policemen deputed to accompany him wherever he went joined the volunteers in trying to protect him. Two pulled out their indentity cards to deter the jawans, but were ignored; one even drew his revolver but to no purpose. The lathis began belabouring the men around JP, some of whom were supporting him as he struggled for breath. Some Bihar uniformed policemen nearby thrust their lathis above him to protect him from the blows. A sarvodaya worker from Gaya stood up betweeen the CRP and their target, to be felled with a lathi blow on his head. Nanaji Deshmukh, general secretary of the Jana Sangh, put out his arm to protect JP and had his forearm broken. Glancing blows struck JP on the collar bone, elbow and leg and he fainted. His companions were particularly worried because of his known heart complaint (a specialist had examined him only the previous day), but he revived and while his injured followers were taken to hospital, he refused to call off the demonstration and proceeded towards the house of Finance Minister Daroga Rai. JP was intercepted and ushered into a nearby bus by the local police and taken near his house. But he refused to get down until 10.30 at night, when the protest ended. Graphic photographs of the attack on JP taken by accompanying press photographers gave the lie to Chief Minister Gafoor's statement that nothing untoward had happened, as well as to Mrs Gandhi's attempt to pass off his injuries as the result of a stampede rather than CRP lathi blows. In his letter dated 28 August, 1976, to the people of Bihar describing his experience, JP recalled that "if Shri Nanaji Deshmukh, Shri Haidar Ali and others of the Bihar police deputed to secure my personal safety had not physically intervened, receiving the CRP lathi blows aimed at me, I would have been a dead man on that day. It happened at the instance of the Central Government because I don't think the Bihar Government would have dared to go to such lengths." Protests came from all over the country and from leaders of all opposition parties except, of course, the CPI. But the most significant condemnation of the Bihar Government came from Chandra Shekhar, leader of a left group in the Congress and a member of its supreme executive, the Working Committee. A fortnight later, he invited JP to an informal meeting with about fifty other Congress MPs and leaders. This was interpreted by Mrs Gandhi, who was already suspicious of the group, as being an open threat to her leadership. Seven months later Chandra Shekhar headed the list of select Congressmen who were arrested at dead of night on the eve of the declaration of internal emergency; and thirty months later he became president of the Janata party which swept the Congress from power in New Delhi. But long before the general election in March, 1977, while addressing a mammoth public meeting in Patna on 18 November, 1974, to celebrate his recovery from the injuries and strain of the 4 November protest, JP accepted a reported challenge from Mrs Gandhi to test their differences at the polls. Once again, he showed his political prescience with the remark: "There will be only two parties in this contest—the janta (the people), the students and the youth will be ranged on one side and those opposed to them, like the Congress and the CPI, on the other. I shall not be a candidate in the countest. I shall, however, surely continue to guide the students, the youth and the people."

JP spent the winter months touring the country and was greeted by ever-increasing crowds wherever he went. At the same time, he sponsored meetings of student representation and of opposition party leaders, ranging from the Jana Sangh to the Marxist Communist party, to secure their support for his movement and to coordinate campaigns for electoral reform, eradicating corruption and curbing the continuing price rise. But he rejected a suggestion that he lead or be a member of a united party. A national coordination committee was set up soon after. Except for the Marxists and the Dravida Munnetra Kazhagam (DMK), a regional party limited to Tamil Nadu, all the others who participated—the old Congress, the Jana Sangh, the Bharatiya Lok Dal (BLD) and the Socialists—eventually united to form the Janata Party. The Congress responded with a secret, but highly publicised conclave at Narora in UP and resuscitated several objectives that the party had pledged to achieve many times before. About the only new feature was an attack on Chandra Shekhar for arranging the meeting with JP, and a consensus in favour of a counter-campaign against his movement.

One of the decisions taken by the National Coordination Committee was to stage a massive people's march on Parliament on 6 March, 1975. Before this JP went round the states of Uttar Pradesh, Madhya Pradesh, Rajasthan, Gujarat, Maharashtra and Punjab drumming up support and collecting funds for the movement. The only states in which he encountered open hostility was Haryana, then under the chief ministership of Bansi Lal, one of the toughest and most unscrupulous aides of Mrs Gandhi and her son. While driving from Delhi to address a public meeting at Kurukshetra, the historic Mahabharata battleground, demonstrators waving black flags and shouting, "Go back JP" surrounded his car outside Karnal and some threw stones at it. Later, local citizens told him that most of the demonstrators were recruits from a nearby police training school.

Early in the new year, two by-election victories in Madhya

Pradesh gave further impetus to JP's efforts, and disheartened the Congress. The Govindpuri assembly seat was won by a candidate jointly sponsored by the main opposition parties. An even bigger and more significant victory was won at Jabalpur, where Sharad Yadav, a student leader chosen by the local people's and students' action committees, and supported by the opposition parties, was elected to the Lok Sabha. The defeat hit the Congress particularly hard because Seth Govind Das, the veteran regional party leader and Hindi enthusiast had held the seat not only in all the other parliamentarian elections held after independence, but also to the central legislature under British rule—a period of fifty years. On his death, the ruling party had assumed that his grandson would inherit the votes and so nominated him, but he got less than half the number secured by Yadav. Another development that deepened the anxiety of the Congress leadership was the death, on January 3, of Lalit Narayan Mishra, Minister for Railways in Mrs Gandhi's cabinet and the party's main fund-raiser, of injuries received in a bomb explosion. Mishra was from Bihar and an attempt was made to blame JP's movement for his death, but the fact that he had become very unpopular for the tough measures he took to crush a recent railway strike and that the bomb had exploded at a railway junction, indicated a different motivation.

The representative character and orderly behaviour of the crowds that massed near Parliament House on 6 March, in response to JP's call, was the next move in what had become a highly sensitive war of nerves. Many poured in from nearby states, to be joined by much of Delhi's population, including government servants and their families. A petition presented to Parliament began :"We, the people of India, have gathered here to express solidarity with the struggle of the Bihar people which has come to symbolise the people's aspirations all over the country. When basic principles of public life and good government are allowed to be trampled, it is the people's duty to protest. We march to serve democracy. We pledge ourselves to a total revolution in society which will create a new order of social and economic equality, genuine democracy, and moral values within the Gandhian framework." JP's hand in preparing the petition was obvious.

From now, events moved faster towards a total confrontation. With neither prepared to retreat, it became clear that the political framework could not contain both JP and Mrs Gandhi much longer. The first anniversary of the Bihar movement was celebrated on 18 March and JP issued a new manifesto clarifying his ideas and intentions. These are some extracts:

"My socio-political-economic ideas have been expressed from time to time in my writings, but I may not be able, just by personal influence, to persuade those who may come to power after the next elections in Bihar, to accept and implement them. I cannot hope to succeed where Gandhiji failed. But there is one historical factor to be taken into account, namely, Gandhiji's assassination less than six months after independence. There is no doubt that had he lived for only five years more, he would have awakened and mobilised the masses and the youth to compel the new rulers of India to cut out their high-sounding but empty verbiage and face the reality of India that lived and still lives in her villages and stinking urban slums.

"Without wanting to draw comparisons, I might say that if my life is spared for a few years, it might be possible for me to compel the new rulers of Bihar to come out of their comfortable homes and offices to face the reality of poverty-stricken and backward Bihar. That could be done only if the students' and people's struggle committees were to continue to function and exercise enough influence over their representatives, not only to make them carry out their promises but also to participate actively in the people's continuing revolutionary struggle. Accordingly, the present attempt is to strengthen the struggle committees so that they do not have to depend upon any leadership from above and can continue to function and march forward on their own...

"The Bihar movement is trying to educate and organize the people so that they might, by their own action, change and better their condition of life. This is one aspect of social change to which traditional politics has paid little attention... Unless the people are made conscious of their rights and organized to fight for them, the benefits conferred by law cannot be realised by them. The Bihar movement, through the struggle committees and janata sarkar, is trying to achieve this end..."

In April, JP sought to carry the message of the movement east and south, to West Bengal and Andhra Pradesh and Tamil Nadu, but was not received with the same enthusiasm as in the north. In Calcutta, Congress toughs organized by the Youth Congress leader Priyaranjan Das Munshi, and Minister of State for Information, Subrata Mukherjee, to counterattack and terrorise the Marxists and the Naxalites, prevented JP from addressing a meeting in the university, by surrounding and jumping on his car, and manhandling such respected leaders as Professor Samar Guha, Kshitish Chandra Roychaudhry and Swarajbandhu Bhattacharyya.

At the same time, he tried to correct the impression created by Congress leaders that he was encouraging the armed forces and police to mutiny, clearly a move to discredit him and his lieutenants, as well as preparation for action against them. In an interview in *Everyman's*, he said: "I consider it my duty to explain to the police that while I was not asking them to rebel and they must do their duty, they must not obey orders that are illegal or go against their conscience... I explained to the young men and to the audience generally that the police are their brethren, that the struggle was not against them, that they belonged to the permanent services and would continue to serve the state even when governments change. I further explained that the policemen were only performing their duty and it was not right to alienate them."

But Congress spokesmen returned repeatedly to the charge and he felt it necessary to reiterate his reply in the letter he addressed to his friends in Bihar on 28 August, 1976. It was circulated clandestinely because the emergency was in force. In this, as well as in the diary he kept in prison, published after Mrs Gandhi's fall, he also defended himself against the charge that he was promoting violence. He insisted that the satyagrahis remain peaceful in the face of a degree of police provocation that resulted in the death of at least 150 persons. In Chapra district, where one policeman was killed in retaliation, he had condemned the incident and had sent Rs 5,000 to his widow. He had also apologised to the Speaker of the Bihar Assembly when an MLA was manhandled at its gate. But, in keeping with the distinction he had made between peaceful and non-violent, he obviously did not feel obliged to call off the movement.

Meanwhile, the hearings in Allahabad of the election petition filed by the BLD leader, Raj Narain, against the Prime Minister began to attract public attention. It was evident from the proceedings that there were weak points in Mrs Gandhi's defence. When Justice Jagmohan Lal Sinha insisted that she appear in court it also became clear that he was not overawed by her office. Even so, when his judgment, announced on 12 June, found her guilty and disqualified her from standing for election to Parliament for six years, it created a commotion throughout the country. The charges of which she was found guilty were technically minor—misusing official machinery to facilitate her election—but her defenders overlooked the fact that the court had caught her, and her aides, telling lies and misleading the country. This was the charge that had discredited Richard Nixon and forced him out of the White House. On the same day as the judgment came news of the Congress defeat in the Gujarat elections, another slap in Mrs Gandhi's face since she had personally led the Congress campaign there. All the leading papers suggested that she resign until her appeal was heard by the Supreme Court. But the very seriousness of the reverse seemed to make her more obstinate, and those dependent on her for political survival strove to create the impression that the country could not do without her. Demonstrators were rounded up from neighbouring states and transported free, in Delhi buses, (incidentally disrupting the service) to her door, to appeal to her to stay on. After a few days of indecision made possible by a twenty day stay granted by Justice Sinha to enable her to appeal to the Supreme Court, Mrs Gandhi resolved to stay put, as suggested by Sanjay. JP echoed the reaction of the bulk of those who comprehended the meaning of the judgment by characterising her continuance in office as a "most shameful and cynical performance...Having been found guilty of corrupt practices, she has compounded her guilt by deciding to continue as Prime Minister without any legal or moral right to the office." But the bulk of the ruling party could not do without her. Their attitude was summed up by Congress president Deva Kanta Barooah's fascist remark: "India is Indira; Indira is India." Congress leaders, industrialists, academics and others were persuaded to put their signatures to a statement insisting that "Mrs Gandhi continue to be the Prime Minister. It is our firm and considered view that for the integrity, stability and progress of the country, her dynamic leadership is indispensable."

With the opposition campaign to force her to resign gathering momentum, the stage was set for the next act. JP was scheduled to fly to Delhi on June 23 to address a public rally, but at Patna airport found that the regular Indian Airlines flight to Delhi was being inexplicably delayed. After waiting for some hours, he rushed to the railway station and caught a train to the capital. He arrived in time to address a public meeting

The Bihar Movement

organized at short notice by the opposition parties on the evening of June 25, where he joined Morarji Desai and other speakers in demanding the resignation of the Prime Minister and reiterating, among other things, his appeal to soldiers and policemen not to obey illegal orders. The public was asked to participate in a week-long satyagraha campaign from June 29 which would include taking daily processions to Mrs Gandhi's residence and courting arrest there. Then, fatigued after a long and arduous day, JP returned to the Gandhi Peace Foundation and went to bed.

CHAPTER FOURTEEN

DESPAIR AND HOPE

AT THREE in the morning of 26 June 1975, Radhakrishna, Secretary of the Gandhi Peace Foundation, woke JP to inform him that the police had come to arrest him. They had arrived an hour earlier, but he had persuaded them to let JP sleep a little longer because he was tired after the previous day's exertions. It did not take long to pack JP's few personal belongings. But, informed about the arrest by telephone, three of his closest sympathisers in the ruling party—Chandra Shekhar, Mohan Dharia and Krishan Kant, all members of Parliament—were able to see him before he was driven away. Chandra Shekhar accompanied him to the police station, to be informed that he, too, was under arrest. Before being taken into custody, JP was heard to quote a Sanskrit saying, *Vinasha kale viperita buddhi*, similar in meaning to the English phrase, "Those whom the gods wish to destroy, they first make mad." But he was considerably shaken to find how much he had miscalculated Mrs Gandhi's reactions and decisions when he learned of the full range of dictatorial measures she had taken under the guise of an internal emergency. The impact is described vividly in a diary he kept in detention. The diary, the letters to the Prime Minister kept with it and his subsequent letter to the people of Bihar, together provide an insight into his thinking and rethinking, his analysis of Mrs Gandhi's temperament, the objectives and limitations of the movement he was leading and other major issues.

The letter to the people of his home state recounts the circumstances of his arrest baldly and unemotionally, but because it was written more than a year later, when he had realised the crippling nature of the sickness he had contracted in detention,

Despair and Hope

his suspicions about the Government's motives become evident much earlier than in the diary. The letter is in Hindi. "At the Gandhi Peace Foundation, where I was staying, I was arrested on 26 June at about 3 A.M.," he told his people. "From there I was taken by car to Sohna in Haryana and detained in a rest house (part of a tourist complex there). On reaching Sohna, I realised that Shri Morarji Desai had also been arrested and brought there. We were detained in the same rest house but were kept apart and not allowed to meet. I requested the police officer who was the common jailor for both of us to let us meet at least at meal times, but the request was turned down.

"I was at the rest house for only three days. During these three days, the doctors who examined me discovered that I had a heart ailment. That was the first time I was found to be suffering from a heart disease. I had never been a heart patient before" (though he had been found to have a murmer of the heart while convalescing at Vellore): "My health had also been generally satisfactory before I was imprisoned. But within three days of my arrest and detention, something was found physically wrong with my heart. So, the doctors sent me to the All-India Institute of Medical Sciences in New Delhi for further examination. Apparently, the doctors wanted a second opinion on their diagnosis. Some of the experts at the Medical Institute like Dr Sujoy B. Roy (who has since passed away) and Dr M.L. Bhatia were known to me. I had also undergone treatment under Dr Bhatia. I was kept at the Medical Institute for two days then flown to Chandigarh in an Indian Air Force plane. My new place of detention was the Post-Graduate Institute of Medical Education and Research at Chandigarh from where I was ultimately released on 12 November 1975."

Although begun nearly four weeks after his arrest, the first entry in JP's prison diary reveals a greater degree of despair and self-blame for his failure to foresee how far Mrs Gandhi could go towards authoritarian rule to remain in office, than caused by any previous miscalculation. But despair does not imply surrender, self-abasement or even rejection of militancy. This is clear from the letter he wrote to the Prime Minister the same day. In fact, the contrast between the two documents brings out an aspect of JP's personality that was never so noticeable, or possibly had not developed to the same extent, before —a difference between personal feelings and public appearance. Possibly, this had developed owing to the essentially lonely life he had led after Prabhavati's death.

The prison diary begins on 21 July 1975, with:

"My world lies in shambles all around me. I am afraid I shall not see it put together again in my life-time. Maybe my nephews and nieces will see that. Maybe.

"Here was I trying to widen the horizons of our democracy. Trying to do it mainly by involving the people more intimately and continuously in the processes of democracy. This in two ways. One, by creating some kind of machinery through which there could be a measure of consultation with the people in the setting up of candidates. Two, by providing a machinery . . . through which the people could keep a watch on their representatives and demand good and honest performance from them. These were the two drops of essence that I wanted to distil out of all the clang and clamour of the Bihar movement. And here am I ending up with the death of democracy.

"Where have my calculations gone wrong? (I almost said 'our' calculations, but that would be wrong. I must bear the full, the whole responsibility). In assuming that a Prime Minister in a democracy would use all the normal and abnormal laws to defeat a peaceful democratic movement, but would not destroy democracy itself and substitute for it a totalitarian system. I could not believe that even if the Prime Minister wanted to do it, her senior colleagues and her party, which has had such high democratic traditions, would permit it. But the unbelievable has happened. . ."

Despair and Hope

The entry for 21 July ends on what, for JP, was an unusual note of bitterness, occasioned presumably by the silence of and even support given to Mrs Gandhi by intellectuals and academics who previously had been most vociferous in backing him. "I wonder," he wrote, "what all those ladies and gentlemen are saying now who used to tell me that I was the only 'hope' for the country. Are they invoking curses on my head for bringing about this terrible doom? I should not be surprised. They may even be saying that shemmed in from all sides as Mrs Gandhi was, she could not but act in the manner she has." In spite of these doubts, however, he goes on to conclude: "But I hope there are some people at least, particularly among the young, who may still be loyal to me and to the cause I represented. They are the hope of the future. India will arise from the grave, no matter how long it may take."

There is no hint of doubt or weakness in his letter to Mrs Gandhi, as is clear from the following extracts, but only a touch of nostalgia and regret over the course she had taken:

Dear Prime Minister,

I am appalled at press reports of your speeches and interviews. (The very fact that you have to say something every day to justify your action implies a guilty conscience.) Having muzzled the press and every kind of public dissent, you continue with your distortions and untruths without fear of criticism or contradiction. If you think that in this way you will be able to justify yourself in the public eye and damn the Opposition to political perdition, you are sorely mistaken. If you doubt this, you may test it by revoking the emergency, restoring to the people their fundamental rights, restoring the freedom of the press, releasing all those whom you have imprisoned or detained for no other crime than performing their patriotic duty. Nine years, Madam, is not a short period of time for the people, who are gifted with a sixth sense, to have found you out...

As I am the villain of the piece, let me put the record straight. This may be of no interest to you—for all your distortion and untruth are wilful and deliberate—but at least the truth would have been recorded.

About the plan to paralyse the government. There was no such plan and you know it. Let me state the facts.

Of all the states of India it was in Bihar alone where there was a people's movement. But there too, according to the Chief Minister's many statements it had fizzled out long ago, if it had ever existed. But the truth is—and you should know if your ubiquitous Intelligence has served you right—that it was spreading and percolating deep down in the countryside. Until the time of my arrest, "janta sarkars" were being formed from the village upwards to the Block level. Later on, the process was to be taken up, hopefully, to the district and state level.

If you have cared to look into the programme of the janta sarkars, you would have found that for the most part it was constructive, such as: regulating the public distribution system, checking corruption at the lower levels of administration, implementing the land reform laws, settling disputes through the age-old custom of conciliation and arbitration, assuring a fair deal to harijans, curbing such social evils as *tilak* and *dahez*, etc. There was nothing in all this that by any stretch of the imagination could be called subversive. Only where the janta sarkars were solidly organized were such programmes as non-payment of taxes taken up. At the peak of the movement in urban areas an attempt was made for some days, through dharna and picketing, to stop the working of government offices. At Patna whenever the Assembly opened, attempts were made to persuade the Members to resign and to prevent them peacefully from going in. All these were calculated programmes of civil disobedience, and thousands of men and women were arrested all over the State.

If all this adds up to an attempt to paralyse the Bihar government, well, it was the same kind of attempt as was made during the freedom struggle through non-cooperation and satyagraha to paralyse the British government. But that was a government established by force, whereas the Bihar government and the legislature are both constitutionally established bodies. What right has anyone to ask an elected government and elected legislature to go? This is one of your favourite questions. But it has been answered umpteen times by competent persons, including well-known constitutional lawyers. The answer is that in a democracy the people do have the right to ask for the resignation of an elected government if it has gone corrupt and has been misruling. And if there is a legislature that persists in supporting such a government it, too, must go, so that the people might choose better representatives...

Be that as it may, except for Bihar, there was no movement of its kind in any other state of India. In U.P. though satyagraha had started in April, it was far from becoming a people's movement. In some other states though struggle committees had been formed, there seemed to be no possibility of a mass movement anywhere. And as the general election to the Lok Sabha was drawing near, the attention of the Opposition parties was turned more towards the coming electoral struggle than to any struggle involving civil disobedience.

Thus, the plan of which you speak, the plan to paralyse the government, is a figment of your imagination, thought up to justify your totalitarian measures.

But suppose I grant you for a minute, for argument's sake, that there was such a plan, do you honestly believe that your erstwhile colleague, the former Deputy Prime Minister of India, and Chandra Shekhar, a member of the Congress Working Committee, were also a party to it? Then why have they also been arrested and many others like them?

No, dear Prime Minister, there was no plan to paralyse the government. If there was any plan, it was a simple, innocent and short-time plan to continue until the Supreme Court decided your appeal. It was this plan that was announced at the Ramlila grounds by Nanaji Deshmukh on 25 June and which was the subject matter of my speech that evening. The programme was for a selected number of persons to offer satyagraha before or near your residence in support of the demand that you should step down until the Supreme Court's judgment on your appeal. The programme was to continue for seven days in Delhi, after which it was to be taken up in the states. And, as I have said above, it was to last only until the judgment of the Supreme Court. I do not see what is subversive or dangerous about it. In a democracy the citizen has an inalienable right to civil disobedience when he finds that other channels of redress or reform have dried up. It goes without saying that the satyagrahi willingly invites and accepts his lawful punishment. This is the new dimension added to democracy by Gandhi. What an irony that it should be obliterated in Gandhi's own India.

It should be noted—and it is a very important point—that even this programme of satyagraha would not have occurred to the Opposition had you remained content with quietly clinging on to your office. But you did not do it. Through your henchmen you had rallies and demonstrations organized in front of your residence begging you not to resign. You addressed these rallies and, justifying your stand, advanced spurious arguments and heaped calumny on the head of the Opposition. An effigy of the High Court Judge was burnt before your residence and posters appeared in the city suggesting some kind of link between the judge and the CIA. When such despicable happenings were taking place every day, the Opposition had no alternative but to counteract the mischief. And how did it decide to do it? Not by rowdyism but by orderly satyagraha, self-sacrifice. It was this "plan" and not any imaginary plan to paralyse the government that has aroused your ire and cost the people their liberties, and dealt a death-blow to their democracy.

And why has the freedom of the press been suppressed? Not because the Indian press was irresponsible, dishonest or anti-government. In fact, nowhere, under conditions of freedom, is the press more responsible, reasonable and fair than it has been in India. The truth is that your anger against it was aroused because, on the question of your resignation after the High Court's judgment, some of the papers took a line that was highly unpalatable to you. And when, on the morrow of the Supreme Court judgment, all the metropolitan papers, including the wavering *Times of India*, came out with well-reasoned and forceful editorials advising you to quit, freedom of the press became too much for you to stomach. That cooked the goose of the Indian press, and you struck your deadly blow. It staggers one's imagination to think that so valuable a freedom as freedom of the press, the very life-breath of democracy, can be snuffed out because of the personal pique of a Prime Minister. . .

You are reported to have said that democracy is not more important than the nation. Are you not presuming too much, Madam Prime Minister? You are not the only one who cares for the nation. Among those whom you have detained or imprisoned there are many who have done much more for the nation than you. And every one of them is as good a patriot as yourself. So, please do not apply salt to our wounds by lecturing to us about the nation.

Moreover, it is a false choice that you have formulated. There is no choice between democracy and the nation. It was for the good of the nation that the people of India declared in their Constituent Assembly on 26 November 1949, that "We, the people of India having solemnly resolved to constitute India into a Sovereign Democratic Republic. . .give to ourselves this

Constitution." That democratic Constitution cannot be changed into a totalitarian one by a mere ordinance or a law of Parliament. That can be done only by the people of India themselves in their new Constituent Assembly, especially elected for that specific purpose. If Justice, Liberty, Equality and Fraternity have not been rendered to "all its citizens" even after a quarter of a century of signing of that Constitution, the fault is not that of the Constitution or of democracy but of the Congress party that has been in power in Delhi all these years. It is precisely because of that failure that there is so much unrest among the people and the youth. Repression is no remedy for that. On the other hand, it only compounds the failure.

I, no doubt, see that the papers are full these days of reports of new policies, new drives, show of new enthusiasm. Apparently you are trying to make up for lost time, that is to say, you are making a show of doing here and now what you failed to do in nine years. But your twenty points will go the same way as your ten points did and the "stray thoughts." But I assure you this time the people will not be fooled. And I assure you of another thing too: a party of self-seekers and spineless opportunists and *jee huzurs* such as the Congress, alas, has become, can never do anything worthwhile. . .

I have written the above in utter frankness without mincing words. I have done so not out of anger or so as to get even with you in words. No, that would be a show of impotence. Nor does it show any lack of appreciation for the care that is being taken of my health. I have done it only to place the naked truth before you, which you have been trying to cover up and distort.

Having performed this unpleasant duty, may I conclude with a few parting words of advice? You know I am an old man. My life's work is done. And after Prabha's going I have nothing and no one to live for. My brother and nephew have their family and my younger sister—the elder died years ago—has her sons and daughters. I have given all my life, after finishing education, to the country and asked for nothing in return. So, I shall be content to die a prisoner under your regime.

Would you listen to the advice of such a man? Please do not destroy the foundations that the Fathers of the Nation, including your noble father, had laid down. There is nothing but strife and suffering along the path that you have taken. You inherited a great tradition, noble values and working democracy. Do not leave behind a miserable wreck of all that. It would take a long time to put all that together again. For it would be put together again, I have no doubt...

JAYAPRAKASH

As his loneliness and sense of self-doubt grew under confinement, JP returned again and again to the reasons for his miscalculating the Prime Minister's authoritarian response to the Bihar movement and the objectives for which it had been launched; the first an attempt to determine his own responsibility for what had happened, the second to justify what he had done. The conflict deepened and led to moods of depression as the gloom of the emergency increased and the prospects of release from authoritarian rule appeared to become more and more remote. His environment only made things worse. He was confined for much of the time to a small hospital room in Chandigarh and could walk only in the closed corridor leading to it, with police guards at either end. The circumstances are described in his letter to the people of Bihar: "My life under detention at Chandigarh is a long story. I would like to say only this much now, that during the 130 and odd days of detention, I remained completely isolated. The total isolation was very painful to me. Of course, doctors, nurses and police officers used to see me but they would only inquire after my health. There was no one with whom I could converse freely. The loneliness was a kind of mental torture."

On 22 July, after four weeks of detention, JP wrote in his diary: "I had always believed that Mrs Gandhi had no faith in democracy, that she was by inclination and conviction a dictator. My belief has tragically turned out to be true... Where then did I go wrong? Events have shown that my mistake was in assuming that, whatever Mrs Gandhi's personal inclination, it would not be possible for her to become a dictator. First I thought that the people would not allow it and she would have no courage to go ahead. Second, I thought that the Congress party... would not let that happen. I still think that popular resistance will grow and gather strength. It will take time."

His contempt for the CPI, rooted in the many occasions that he felt that communist leaders had exploited his credulity and betrayed the country, and the possible role of the Soviet Union gave an extra dimension to his attitude to Mrs Gandhi. This is noted quite frankly in the same entry in his diary: "Of course, quite a number of Congressmen are disguised communists. They will go with Mrs Gandhi to the ultimate end. They have always been enemies of democracy. Behind them is the right (Moscow-oriented) CPI and behind it is Soviet Russia. Russia has backed Mrs Gandhi to the hilt. Because the farther Mrs Gandhi advances on her present course, the more powerful an influence will Russia have over this country. A time may come when, having squeezed the juice out of Mrs Gandhi, the Russians, through the CPI and their Trojan horses within the Congress, will dump her on the garbage heap of history and instal in her place their own men." (Some aspects of Mrs Gandhi's subsequent behaviour and Sanjay's outspoken criticism of communists suggest that they may have been coming to the same conclusion.) "That India, too should become another Pakistan or Bangladesh: What a shame that would be! These countries did not have a Gandhi, a Nehru, a Patel, a Rajendra Prasad, a Maulana Azad, a Rajagopalachari. Will all their work be reduced to ashes? It is difficult to believe it. That is why I said yesterday (in the diary) Indian democracy will arise from its grave."

He returned to the subject on 26 July, after a month in detention : "There must be two plans instead of one. One, to which Indiraji is privy and is made to believe that it is her plan. In this plan, Indiraji is always at the top till death intervenes. The other plan is a Soviet plan which the CPI has been made to believe has emerged from their own brilliant heads. This plan is not known to Indiraji though she might have some private suspicions. It is also not known to the communist stooges in the Congress, except a very few whom the Soviets trust and who by their outward actions have never shown any sympathy for the CPI or even the Soviets..."

On 6 August, the outlook seemed darker: "The expected has happened. Mrs Gandhi has insured herself against a possible adverse judgment of the Supreme Court by amendment of the Representation of the People Act. A drastic constitutional amendment is also expected. All this to complete the dictatorship of the self-appointed saviour of the country. All this is said to be done according to the Constitution. Hitler, too, used the democratic process to establish his fateful dictatorship. Will India also have to go through hell to emerge again from this darkness ? It seems certain now. But the price India will have paid is crippling. May God help her."

The next day, the agony of self-blame (translated from Hindi): 'Total Revolution' is our slogan; future history belongs to us. Will this now remain an irony of history? All *jee huzurs*, cowards and sycophants must be laughing at us. 'They dared to reach the stars, but descended into hell', this is how they must be ridiculing us. But only those who seek to reach the stars have achieved anything in the world, maybe at the cost of their lives. Instead of total revolution, we find today the dark clouds of total counter-revolution, encircling us. It is a feast day for the owls and jackals whose hoots and growls we hear from all sides. But howsoever dark the night may be, the dawn is bound to follow."

At this point, the desire for death is not far: "If social revolution were just to follow the revolutions of nature, there would have been no place for human effort for social progress and change. What then are we to do? The answer is, 'They who raised that slogan and sang that song must offer to sacrifice themselves. And the first to kiss the altar must be the one who was their leader.' Doubts have been set at rest; the decision has been taken. Last night while offering prayers to the goddess Bhagwati, I had asked for a way out of this darkness, and I got it this morning. My mind is now calm and composed." JP had taken a decision to go on an indefinite fast, which was later postponed, and wrote a letter to Mrs Gandhi informing her of the decision, but it was not sent. These decisions referred to in a brief, cryptic entry on August 11: "My earlier decision stands. The letter was not sent. I destroyed it. I will wait for the proper time after seeing how the situation develops."

For three days, JP was obviously trying hard to concentrate on developments outside his isolated hospital room, not on his own fears. He reiterated his views on electoral reform and Gandhian democracy to rebut the Prime Minister's charge that he believed in dictatorship and commented on constitutional arguments. But on 14 August, he returns to his own deteriorating condition: ". . . except for the Director (of the Institute), as soon as any other doctor or one of the nurses enters my room, there follows closely, the jailor or police—(maybe also the IB, Intelligence Branch or CBI, Central Bureau of Investigation)—they are all parked here on the entire floor occupying several rooms—representative (a head sepoy perhaps) who keeps standing at my door all the 24 hours (they take turns)... Thus, while I am in hospital and am being well looked after" (this was written before he became suspicious about his treatment) "and while a number of persons come and go, I am really alone.

Despair and Hope

Every day there is something in the papers that completely upsets me—usually it is Mrs Gandhi's half-truths and lies... Until a few days ago, more precisely till I wrote in these pages that I had decided not to bother to comment upon what Mrs Gandhi chose to say, I used to get so upset that sometimes I had to ring for a dose of a tranquilizer... So this for me is truly solitary confinement. Day and night—except for the times I am taken out for short walks in the enclosed, stuffy corridor of this floor—I have to keep within my room." He went on to contrast the way he was being treated with the relatively humane conditions in which he had been detained under British rule.

On 15 August, Independence Day, he asked: "...Is anything left of that democracy (envisaged in the Constitution) today? All this appears to be so unreal and dreamlike that the President and the Prime Minister have to reassure the people again and again that the emergency is a temporary affair." Here JP reiterated his faith that India's people and especially her youth would not allow democracy to be liquidated. To justify this, he stressed India's size and diversity and recalled that "history is witness to the fact that the effort to govern the whole of India from a single centre was never fully successful... This was the state of affairs even when there was no concept of democracy based on adult franchise, or of civil liberties and rights of every common citizen...I do not find any such personal quality in Indiraji or in her party as to believe that her autocratic rule over this vast land will continue for long."

Before concluding for the day, JP reiterated an objective for which he had been working without much success, and in doing so gave another instance of his ability to anticipate the fusion of emotional and political factors that brings about revolutionary change. "If the Opposition parties had been united," he noted, "the Congress rule would have ended long ago. I hope the Opposition, having passed through the fire of dictatorship, will unite now. In fact, one of the reasons that contributed to the proclamation of emergency was that, after the victory of the Janata front in Gujarat, Mrs Gandhi felt that there was a possibility of Opposition unity at the national level, in which case she might not win the next election to the Lok Sabha. Moreover, the impact of the Bihar movement was spreading to other States. In such a situation, she might herself have decided that her interest lay in destroying democracy itself. However, as would be clear from what I have said above, she will never succeed in this satanic attempt."

Apart from these insights, the most valuable thoughts recorded in the diary concerned the Bihar movement, its objectives and the key importance of struggle, of organized pressure from outside the formal democratic structure, to achieve the breakthrough in all seven aspects of life—social, economic, political, cultural, ideological or intellectual, educational and spiritual—that he termed Total Revolution. JP clarified his thinking on the subject, and of those who read the diary, to an extent that may not have been possible if he had not been forced to focus on it to save himself from despair. He identified the basic issues on 23 August by noting that the conditions in which nine-tenths of the population of the country—small and marginal landowners and the landless, the backward classes and the harijans—existed, continued to be miserable. Meanwhile, state capitalism, with no element of true socialism in it, had multiplied inefficiency, waste and corruption. The educational system remained basically the same as during British rule: a system of "class education designed as an escalator to reach the top. In most of the country, customs, manners, beliefs and superstitions had not changed, while there had been a steady decline in political, public and business morality. Poverty was growing, with more than 40 per cent of the people below the poverty line.

The underlying question he then poses is: "Can the picture

be fundamentally altered through the ordinary democratic process? Even if the Opposition wins, will the picture change?" And he answers: "I fear, no. Laws will be passed and applied, moneys will be spent—even if all this is done, possibly without corruption creeping in, will the structure, the system, the 'order' of our society change?" He did not think so. For instance, laws had not prevented the system of dowry ruining many families and the lives of many girls. So he concluded: "There is no remedy but a vigorous social movement, a peaceful struggle against the evil. Likewise, the implementation of land reforms, homestead tenancy legislation, removal of corruption in the administration, etc. All this required a mass awakening and a mass struggle. The youth, including the students, must naturally be in the vanguard."

To bring about a systemic change in society, a revolution in every sphere and aspect of society became even harder when it had to be brought about peacefully, without impairing the democratic structure of society. "Put in this way, the most legalistic and constitutionalist democrat would agree that all this could never be accomplished if the functioning of democracy were restricted to elections, legislation, planning and administrative execution. There must also be people's direct action. This action would almost certainly comprise, among other things, civil disobedience, peaceful resistance, non-cooperation —in short, satyagraha in its widest sense."

He recalled Chandra Shekhar (who later became the Janata party president), asking him if the situation would change if the Congress was replaced by an opposition government. His answer was "that the movement's only aim was not only to change government in Bihar, but much more, which I had 'capsuled' (if I may coin this word) in the term revolution. The movement would go on, which in itself would be a powerful guarantee of the opposition government always being on its toes and it would go faster and smoother because the new government would give its full cooperation... The upshot of what I have been saying is that the people's movement of the type I am visualizing here can proceed either in cooperation or in confrontation with the government concerned."

Why had it not been possible for Congress governments to cooperate with such movements? JP found the answer in corruption: "Mrs Gandhi's own conduct in collecting crores from rich businessmen for party and election management," he noted, "is a piece of political corruption that has completely destroyed the moral sensibilities of most power-seeking Congressmen." Money had been collected earlier, too, "but the scale of operations was comparatively small and most of the money was accounted for... Nor were business bargains struck in the process so shamelessly corrupt as those of which one has heard in Mrs Gandhi's time."

Would opposition parties behave any differently? Returning to the issue a week after he mentioned it in relation to Chandra Shekhar's question, his analysis shows greater clarity. "Having once joined the movement," he wrote, "no doubt to exploit it for party and election purposes (which is in the very nature of political parties), they find themselves not only committed to the final goal of total revolution but also being radicalised in the process of the struggle... The only exceptions are places where only one party holds sway, and the non-party among students, citizens and the local sarvodaya workers are weak; the party in question has in that case identified its party interests with the interests of the struggle. It was precisely with a view to strengthening the non-party forces that I had been busy organizing a new volunteer force of non-party youths and students called Chhatra Yuvak Sangharsha Vahini."

But could the psychological climate necessary for struggle be created at will? Although the preconditions for a social struggle were present in poverty, unemployment, mis-education etc., JP noted that "still there is need for a spark to kindle the fires

of struggle, to set alight the dry tinder-box of Indian society."
The emergency had created a new situation, but—unsentimentally for once—he wrote: "The longer the fighters are kept in prison, the better it would be for the resumption of the struggle."

Even with the rigours of the emergency reaching their peak, JP felt that Mrs Gandhi was committed to hold elections; though this would be when she was satisfied that the opposition was demoralized and the people dazzled by her 20-point programme. "Whenever that moment comes," he again predicted correctly, "the election date will be announced and the detenus released."

Returning to the subject next day, he felt that the Gujarat and Bihar movements had shown that they could grow out of a comparatively minor agitation. From this viewpoint, the Gujarat movement "was a path-finder in India's march towards democracy. . . . The Gujarat movement established for the firs time in India the primacy of the people, going over the heads of organized parties and asserting their will."

A few days later, he turned his attention to the "prevailing system" in India and its philosophy: he found it dominated by the small, economically better-off section, "a tiny part of them quite affluent in the Western style-of-living sense. . . . If there is a system it is made of these elements and the system's philosophy is that of the educated and economic elite. The elite from the rural areas are being constantly sucked into the urban areas.

"What is the philosophy of the system? To have more of what they have, to climb higher up and, on the radical fringes, (socialist, communist etc.) to see that more persons have what they have—i.e., spread the benefit. All politics, all education, all privileges are confined to this tiny layer of society at the top—not necessarily all capitalists, but all privileged. . . In India, this tiny layer of the elite, barring rare individuals, wants more modern technology, more industrialization, more mechanization put chemicalization of agriculture. That is the ethos of modernism in India."

Although no longer a disciple of Acharya Vinoba Bhave, JP remained sensitive to anything he said or did that reflected on his activities. He mulled over some of the differences between them in the diary. He recalled, for instance, that Vinoba had advised him against waging a struggle against the government n the course of his struggle against economic and social injusitice. The reason given by the Acharya was surprisingly chauvinistic: that with the United States arming Pakistan and China also helping her—"more with words than military hardware," noted JP—it was not advisable to weaken the government. "But what do we have now?" asked JP. "Not a war with Pakistan but a deliberate, preplanned and ghastly murder of Indian democracy. Vinobaji had not given a hint of this. I wonder if he considers that a totalitarian dictatorship is a healthy course of discipline, a sort of fire of purification which the country and particularly hotheads like me, Morarji Desai, Siddharaj (Dhadda, president of the Sarva Seva Sangh, who was also in detention), and a host of others must pass so that India becomes strong enough to face her enemies and also make progress towards moral, material and spiritual fulfilment." On 11 September JP wrote: "Today is Vinoba's birthday. He completes 80 years of his life today. May he live for a hundred years!" But he was not so generous about the Congress leaders who used the occasion to lionise Vinoba and emphasize the differences between him and JP. "It is all so disgustingly cunning," he noted. "Mrs Gandhi's plane dash to Vinoba, her overnight stay at the ashram and now these fulsome celebrations in Delhi. . . . " On 2 October, Mahatma Gandhi's birth anniversary, he stressed the difference between Gandhi's activist philosophy and Vinoba's "experiment of 'action' in the form of 'inaction'." JP was less sarcastic about Vinoba in his letter to the people of Bihar. He minimized the difference between them. "Actually there is no big difference of opinion or conception on the basic questions facing our people," he wrote. "The differences are only about the approach, the mode of thinking. You know Vinoba is a saint. He is a spiritual man. He approaches every question from a spiritual point of view. I look at them from the social point of view. So differences are natural in our methods of working. Such differences lead to differences of opinion between friends, and they have occurred. But today our country is in a dangerous situation and to get over it there is need for the spiritual leadership of Vinoba Bhave."

As had happened so often before, floods in his home state had always moved JP. The major flood reported in the newspapers on 27 August, 1975, impelled him to send a message to Mrs Gandhi, followed by a letter appealing to be let out on parole to be able to organize relief. He went to the extent of saying that, "I would consider it immoral and impolitic to exploit the period of freedom allowed to me for any political purpose." But his appeal went unheeded.

Another event that moved him greatly while under detention was the murder of President Mujibur Rahman of Bangladesh and members of his family. But his anguish for the family did not blind the democrat in him. "But this is the result of the personal and party dictatorship Mujib had established," he wrote in his diary on 16 August. "Rumours were thick in Delhi, at that time, that the whole strategy followed by Mujib had been worked out at Delhi with Mujib's trusted men. At that time Mujib also gave out excuses similar to those being given now by Mrs Gandhi. It was also rumoured at the time of the Mujib coup that India, too, was to go the Bangladesh way, that is, if Mrs Gandhi had her way, India is half-way today between democracy and the Mujib dictatorship."

The final entries in JP's diary reveal how sudden, painful and suspicious was the onset of the illness that led to the malfunctioning of his kidneys and brought him near death's door. On 26 September, he wrote that he had completed three months of detention, but the days were passing fairly quickly. A week earlier, he had been regarded as well enough to be moved to a cottage in the grounds of the Chandigarh institute. No nurses would be in attendance and the doctors would drop in occasionally. "This is one step towards normal health," he had written in his diary. He was alert enough to complete reading the third volume of Bertrand Russell's autobiography, and be impressed by it. He was also happy and hopeful when Sugata Dasgupta, Director of the Gandhian Institute of Studies in Varanasi, that he had set up, appeared in his room. He interpreted Dasgupta's visit as an indication that the worst of the emergency was over.

He was too weak with pain to write on 28 September. But he was able to describe his agony briefly the following day. "Yesterday was a bad day for me," he wrote. "In the morning as I sat on the water closet there was a terrible pain in the stomach. At first I thought it would pass off. But it continued and became more severe. I began to perspire copiously, felt faint and very weak. Had difficulty in getting up, washing and returning to my bed. I asked for Dr Kalara to be called and also Dr Chihuttani (director of the institute) to be informed. The pain continued for hours. The doctors gave medicines. Was in bed the whole day. Took only liquids and at night a little rice with curds. The diagnosis is some infection. Whatever it be, this was the first experience of its kind in my life. Because of the profuse perspiration and pain and weakness, I thought at first I had a heart attack—but the pain was in the lower abdomen. Heart, BP (blood pressure) etc. were normal. The ECG was taken and nothing new was found. Today I feel much better. Just had a 20-minute walk in the lawn—6.30 p.m."

There was a 10-day gap before the next paroxysm, with no apparent change in JP's reactions to events and visitors. A newspaper report of a speech by Jagjivan Ram describing Mrs Gandhi's leadership as vital, attracted his disgust. President Sadat's speech in Cairo criticizing the Soviet role in Egypt drew the comment: "Is there anyone in the ruling circles in our country who can speak with forthrightness and boldness...God knows how deep the Russians have penetrated into our decision-making and vital organs of government and polity." On 2 October, the 106th anniversary of Mahatma Gandhi's birth, he was moved to comment (in Hindi), "Bapu, I offer my salutations at your feet." He was caustic about the role of the intellectuals. "For some years now," he noted, "the intellectuals of the country have been feeling that by deviating from Gandhi's path, India committed a great blunder. But these very intellectuals, or others similar to them in Jawaharlal's time, looked upon Gandhiji as a conservative and praised the 'modern' outlook of Nehru. Mrs Gandhi, who has mastered the art of deception, has often claimed that she is only on the path of Gandhiji. Perhaps she will express similar sentiment even today during his birthday celebrations. But all this is fraud. . ." Next day, he was greatly moved and saddened by reading about the death of Kamaraj, the Tamil leader who had broken the hold of the Brahmin caste on southern politics. Noting Mrs Gandhi's decision to attend Kamaraj's funeral and thus strengthen her claim that he belonged to her faction of the Congress, and recalling Jawaharlal's failure to attend the funeral of former President Rajendra Prasad, he commented acidly, "For the Nehrus it seems politics decide everything!" He was heartened by further visits by Sugata Dasgupta, who was to convey his views to P. N. Dhar, Secretary to the Prim Minister.

But soon after Dasgupta's last visit on 8 October, the agonising pain returned. Writing with evident difficulty two days later, he recalled: "Healthwise, 8th was again a bad day for me. Mostly intestinal trouble. Stomach felt like bursting from within, even though it was soft to the touch from the outside. No appetite. Constipation—not even gas passing. Had 99.2 temperature in the evening. There seems to be some infection in the intestine and inflammation... Feel much better today, though weak and exhausted."

Next day (11 October) was JP's 73rd birthday. "May God grant me the wisdom and the will to devote whatever time is left for me to the service of the country and the people. That is the only way I have known to serve God," he wrote and was pleased and surprised when the superintendent of the jail, Sardar Mohinder Singh, gave him a large bouquet of flowers. On 20 October, the report of a relatively outspoken speech by Sheikh Abdullah made him hope "we shall hear more such voices. For the present, however, there is the silence of the grave in the entire country."

Then the pain was back, worse than ever. On 29 October, he managed to write: "Have gone through hell these last days—days (of) continuous pain in the lower abdominal region. Felt miserable. All kinds of investigations were done but nothing has been found. Yet the pain, though less than before, continues. Constipation—'trifala' does not work any more. Vomiting last night and this morning too. Have no appetite. There is total aversion to food."

Three days later: "The abdominal pain continues until this day. No appetite, and aversion to food. No motion. Was moved to the hospital (the same room in which I was before) on 31 October night. Feel miserable and depressed due to this constant pain...." On 4 November, JP wrote: "Feel better today. Abdominal pain is much less." The last item in the diary was inscribed the next day. It was an appreciative note on Satyavrat's commentary on the *Gita*, which he finished reading that day.

JP was released from detention on 12 November and, four days later, flown to the All India Institute of Medical Sciences

Despair and Hope

in New Delhi, where he had been taken after his arrest four and a half months earlier. To the few friends who were able to see him, it was evident that he had been freed because he was on the brink of death. His face was ashen, he could hardly lift his head from the pillow and was too weak to recognize even those he knew well. But even then, the hospital authorities apparently failed to detect the extent to which his kidneys were damaged. At his brother Raja's insistence, he was flown to Bombay on 22 November and admitted to Jaslok Hospital. It was then that the doctors diagnosed that only regular dialysis could keep him alive. The suspicion that he had been poisoned, though not necessarily with the connivance of the doctors, was hard to eradicate thereafter.

CHAPTER FIFTEEN

THE CONTINUING SEARCH

On 25 November 1975, exactly six months after his arrest, JP was connected to an artificial kidney machine to clean his blood of the impurities that his kidneys could no longer remove. "Dialysis" became a familiar word throughout the country, though not many knew precisely what it meant, or how long and painful a process it could be. The censored press could report only that he had been put on dialysis and that his general condition remained the same as before. But little by little, the picture emerged of a man in his seventies, crippled by a disease that would never be cured, living on a treatment that kept him tied to a machine for seven hours a day, three times a week, undergoing the pain of having needles planted in an artery and vein to enable the blood in his body to be passed through a machine, the after-effects varying from day to day, too weak to stand up unaided—and yet continuing to think, and discuss with others, how to save the country from the ever-tightening clutches of dictatorship. It seemed an impossible task—now and then he too seemed to lose hope—but he was kept alive by the faith that his countrymen, the poor and illiterate among whom he had worked rather than the urban intellectuals whose commitment to freedom had been exposed as skin-deep, would somehow overturn the increasingly personal rule of Mrs Gandhi and her son. Not even the specialists could be sure just how long dialysis could keep him going. The effect varied from individual to individual. To make things worse, he suffered a mild heart attack two weeks after the dialysis began and had to be moved into the intensive care unit of Jaslok Hospital. But he recovered and progressed enough to shift to his brother Raja's flat in Colaba, from where the sea was visible, and return to the hospital on Mondays, Wednesdays and Fridays for dialysis.

But he could not think only of himself. He had to return to Bihar, where the movement he had guided had touched off widespread repression. So in May 1976, his friends and admirers started a fund that would meet the cost of buying a dialyser unit and installing it in his modest home in Patna. The response was immediate. Rs 330,000 was collected in small donations, but not quickly enough to expose once more the innocence of his nature (which had led his family to nickname him "Baul" in his childhood) when faced with the craftiness of a political expert like Mrs Gandhi. She promptly offered to contribute Rs 90,000—the estimated cost of the machine—and he accepted, interpreting it as an attempt at reconciliation. But soon, the use made by the official publicity media of the acceptance of the contribution as indication that JP himself did not feel that the Prime Minister was responsible for his illness or the other excesses of the emergency, and the scandalized reaction of his own supporters, made him realise his mistake. The contribution had not cost her anything personally because it came from the Prime Minister's National Relief Fund. So, he belatedly turned down the contribution with a letter to Mrs Gandhi (addressed, "Dear Indiraji") explaining that more than the amount required had been collected and he did not want to take money from the relief fund when many relief projects were awaiting funds. The censor banned publication of his letter, but full publicity was given to her response in the form of a comment from an "official spokesman." He was quoted as remarking that "it was strange that while there was no hesitation about accepting donations from foreign sources for the purpose (in fact all foreign contributions were returned) and earlier from businessmen, including those against whom cases are pending (a dig at his friend and Bombay host, Ramnath Goenka), there should be compunctions about a contribution from the national fund." But JP never learnt from such experiences; he was no politician and fell into similar traps again and again.

The incident was also another example of his desire never to reject a possible move towards reconciliation—a lesson taught by Mahatma Gandhi who was, however, much shrewder in detecting political motivations. He had earlier blessed an attempt by the Socialist leader, N.G. Goray, one of the few not to be detained, to break the ice, and even addressed a covering note to Mrs Gandhi. There was no response.

JP's efforts to unite the non-communist Opposition parties were more successful, though they seemed equally theoretical since hardly anyone believed that Mrs Gandhi would ever give Opposition parties an opportunity to fight a fair election, or that the bulk of the voters would feel strongly enough to take the risk of voting against the ruling party. In this task, however, he was helped by the opportunity that the Prime Minister inadvertently provided for lengthy discussions between party leaders by detaining most of them in two jails, Rohtak and Ambala, between which sympathetic jail officials provided communication. On 25 May 1976, JP was able to announce the formation of a national party consisting of members of the Old Congress, the Jana Sangh, the Bharatiya Lok Dal and the Socialists. After this, his calendar consisted of bursts of activity designed to remove jealousies and misunderstandings between the integrating parties, and at the same time to reinvigorate the student and youth movement, especially in Bihar. As before, he had a dual objective: to strengthen the functioning of parliamentary democracy and also to keep alive the sources of popular agitation and movements. The rigours of the emergency did not modify his belief that outside pressure was essential to prevent formal democracy from becoming a process for the tiny elite groups of the country to exchange power and preserve the status quo while the poverty-stricken mass of the population continued to be exploited. In between, he would find himself back in hospital because of exhaustion or disappointment and the need to change the painful place where the dialyser was connected to his blood vessels.

JP was, perhaps, the only leader of any stature in the country who was not taken completely by surprise by Mrs Gandhi's broadcast on 18 January, 1977, that general elections to the Lok Sabha would be held in March. Her own colleagues were surprised because only two months earlier the life of the Lok Sabha had been extended a second time, which meant that elections did not have to be held until March 1978. Only ten days earlier, her Defence Minister and close aide of Sanjay, Bansi Lal, had told a public meeting that there was no hurry to hold elections because the country was fully engaged in what he described as "the task of reconstruction and development." In much of northern India, this had meant a campaign of forcible sterilisation, especially of Muslims and Harijans, and a programme of forced eviction of poor shanty-dwellers in Delhi and other major cities.

More surprising than the decision to hold the elections was the fact that they were not rigged and that the curbs on the press and public meetings were eased. Presumably, the intelligence agencies and party leaders misled Mrs Gandhi about how unpopular the Congress party had become by following the feudal custom of not reporting anything unpalatable to the ruler. But, again, JP was not surprised. His faith in the people was strong enough to believe that even the officers and men of the Border Security Force and Central Reserve Police, who could have been used to deter opposition voters, were unhappy enough with the way in which they had been used to suppress popular demonstrations, that they would refuse to allow open rigging. But his confidence that the elections would be relatively free did not prevent him from describing the issue at stake as "democracy versus dictatorship." He flew to Delhi on 22 January to confer with Morarji Desai and other Opposition leaders who had been released. He told a news conference next day that the ruling party obviously calculated that it could not be defeated when it controlled radio and television as well as Samachar, the single national news agency into which the four pre-emergency news agencies had been forcibly united under government pressure. But, he went on to explain, "like all dictatorial groups, they (the ruling party) have a contempt for the people. But today the people cannot be so easily misled. They have learnt the hard way that it is only democratic procedures that protect the rights of the poor." On 24 January, he had to be back in Patna for his session with the dialyser.

On his next visit to Delhi, JP met Jagjivan Ram, whose decision to leave the Congress together with former UP Chief Minister H.N. Bahuguna and form the Congress for Democracy shook the entire organization. On 6 February, both of them addressed a crowd at the Ramlila ground that was bigger than on the last occasion he was there—the evening before the promulgation of the emergency and his arrest.

Reinvigorated by the course of events, JP threw himself into the election campaign. On 21 February, the *Indian Express* published the following account of his travels :

In the evening of a life full of struggle for one cause or another, Jayaprakash Narayan is conducting probably the most strenuous and taxing campaign he has attempted so far, considering his age and the grim handicap of ill-health.

If it was not for the letter "D" marked against several days of his election tour programme, it could match the schedule of any youthful leader in the pink of health.

But the "D" stands for dialysis every Monday, Wednesday and Friday. The regular day-long cleansing of his blood three times a week represents JP's hold on life.

On weekends, when there is a two-day interval between dialysis, the strain is evident by Sunday evening. A longer break could mean rapid collapse.

That does not prevent JP from campaigning every day that is not a D-day. He is now visiting all the major cities in the country. To do this and yet return to Bombay's Jaslok Hospital for dialysis, means a tight travel schedule by air, train and car.

The campaign began with his travelling from Patna, where the dialysis machine paid for by contributions from the public is installed, by train to Calcutta where he addressed a mass meeting last Thursday. From there he flew to Bombay to be in time for dialysis next day.

Problems came up early. The timing of his flight had been advanced by an hour and a half. So he had to cut the meeting short. Worse, there was no one to receive him at Santa Cruz, so he had to take a taxi to reach his brother's flat at the other end of the town.

This weekend, he has covered both Jaipur and Ahmedabad, thanks to convenient flights. At his halts, he spends the morning persuading local Opposition leaders, who may not have worked together before, to cooperate fully. In the afternoon he addresses a mass meeting.

His message is simple. This is the last free election if the Congress is voted back to power.

So far he has stood up to the strain well. He seems buoyed up by the response to and the importance of his mission. Two attendants accompany him to look after his needs—and just in case!

He will give one day to Bombay between dialysis sessions on February 21 and 23. From there his programme is: February 24 by air to Hyderabad, fly back to Bombay for dialysis on February 25. Leave the same evening for Delhi, where after stopping the night he will address a series of meetings in Chandigarh and Punjab on the weekend of February 26 and 27, returning to Delhi in time to catch the last flight to Bombay.

After dialysis next day he flies to Indore on March 1. To return in time for dialysis the next day, he drives to Ratlam in time to catch the Frontier Mail back to Bombay. The other places he visits before returning to Patna on March 7 are Poona (March 3), Bangalore (March 5) and Madras the next day.

From then on, he will concentrate on touring in Bihar and eastern UP if all goes well.

On 20 March, election day in Patna, JP got up at 5 A.M. to make sure that he was one of the first to vote. Counting began that evening and the first phone call from Delhi came at nine to inform him of the trend of voting in Rae Bareli and Amethi, from where Mrs Gandhi and her son were standing. He was heard to remark: "So. The janta (people) are very alert; they have defeated both mother and son. He called the press next day to urge the country's new leadership to move swiftly to provide the clean and responsive government the people had been awaiting so long. He wanted the constitutional and legal powers which Mrs Gandhi and her son had used to set the country on the road to dictatorship to be repealed promptly and the coercive machinery that had been set up to be dismantled. But he did not look particularly happy, and when group after group of enthusiastic students came singing and shouting, "Lok Nayak Zindabad!" he finally sent word asking them not to make so much noise. He went to bed earlier than usual at 8 P.M. The last man he met before retiring, Dr Razi Ahmed of the Gandhi Peace Foundation, suggested that perhaps he was sad about Mrs Gandhi's defeat. This was not impossible, for JP had never quite forgotten his relationship with the Nehru family. But now he replied with a fleeting smile: "No, she fully deserved it," and covering his face with the bedsheet, went to sleep.

He had changed his dialysis schedule to be in Delhi on 23 and 24 March, when the new Prime Minister would be chosen and the new Janata government take office. The main contenders were the Janata chairman, Morarji Desai, and the CFD leader, Jagjivan Ram. Desai had the reputation of being rigid and self-righteous, but those who had met him after his release from detention said he was changed considerably. Ram had always been an astute politician and a sound administrator, but his reputation was not unsullied. A few years earlier, it had been discovered that he had "forgotten" to pay his income tax for ten years. He had also stayed on as the most senior minister in Mrs Gandhi's cabinet during the emergency and had even gone to the extent of moving the resolution to approve it in the autumn session of the Lok Sabha, though this had meant condemning all the men with whom he was now allied, including JP. But had explained after he resigned that it would have done e good for him to have condemned the emergency or t/ith resigned any earlier. He would only have been put in after the others. In fact, if he had not waited to resignions, it Mrs Gandhi was committed to holding general oeen held. was more than possible that they would never) of the Con- When few were able to foresee the complete D that attrac- gress in the north, it was the lure of Babuji' claim to prime ted dissident Cangressmen. This was ministership.

On the 23rd evening it was decid_rence for Prime Minis-
Janata MPs would indicate their _hen announce a consensus
ter to JP and Kripalani who wor (Gandhian) group which had
on this basis. But the sarvoda_a, many socialists and several
campaigned actively for Ja_with the prospect of Jagjivan Ram
others were plainly unhap_So too was Charan Singh. The next
becoming Prime Ministe_bed in Willingdon Hospital he sent a
morning from his sic_y that he would not be able to serve in a
message stating clea_agjivan Ram. When a meeting of MPs was
cabinet headed by_morning, after they had taken a pledge at
called later that

Gandhi Samadhi, it was resolved that no useful purpose would be served by going through the lengthy process of consulting each MP individually. The majority were for Desai. So instead of counting individual ballots, the two elder statesmen resorted to a voice vote. The parliamentary party confirmed the decision. Obviously upset, the CFD declared that it would not merge with the Janata, as was expected earlier, but would support it on merit in Parliament. But JP was not too upset: he was confident that public pressure would keep the bickering leaders together. The ties with the Nehrus, and the manners of a dying era, were not forgotten even in the press of such history-making events. JP broke away from his numerous engagements to speak. Some time with Mrs Gandhi in the hour of her defeat. Not much was said. He was moved, as usual, when he is another's dritress; so apparently, was she.

sympated to Patna. There was much to be done. With a ting up a government in New Delhi, the programme of setting out the State work of non-party people's committees through- doctors decided it should be pushed ahead faster. But the next day, his as soon as possible must be taken to Jaslok Hospital in Bombay new Union Government because blood was clotting the shunt. The him to Bombay, first promptly sent an air force plane to fly interest in the first excitement where he could take only a marginal to fly half-way across the world week of Janata rule, until obliged the United States, for admission to Seattle, on the west coast of preparing patients for extended dialysis to a hospital specialising in

And so on 1 May, when the leaders of the Old Congress, Jana Sangh, BLD and Socialist party, were meeting at a convention to complete the job he had begun—their formal integration into one Janata party—and to accept his choice of Chandra Shekhar to be its first President, JP was flying back, exhausted, on his long flight from Bombay to Seattle. Friction would continue, but his estimate of public pressure proved accurate:

The Continuing Search

Jagjivan Ram enthused the convention by informing it that his Congress for Democracy would integrate with Janata after all. JP's hopes for the future did not centre on the new ruling party. Its victory had not altered his conviction that a real revolution, in which the differences and disparities that impregnated every aspect of the country's socio-economic structure were erased, could not be achieved by governmental action or the paternal plans put together by a westernised elite. It could come only if the poor and under-privileged in the remote villages were made aware of, and organized to insist on, their rights. That was the process of total revolution, not the election to office of one party or other, though a sympathetic government could help accelerate the process.